UNITED METHODIST STUDIES

Basic Bibliographies

Third Edition

Compiled and edited by

Kenneth E. Rowe

ABINGDON PRESS
Nashville
1992

5.35

UNITED METHODIST STUDIES: BASIC BIBLIOGRAPHIES

Compilation copyright © 1982, 1987, 1992 by Abingdon Press.

Library of Congress Cataloging-in-Publication Data

United Methodist studies : basic bibliographies /compiled and ed-
ited by Kenneth E. Rowe. – 3rd ed.
    p.   cm.
  ISBN 0-687-43165-4
  1. Methodist Church – Bibliography.   2. United Methodist
Church (US) – Bibliography.
Z7845.M5U45   1992
[BX8331.2]
016.287'6 – dc20   92-4816
                                                     CIP

Printed in the United States of America
on recycled, acid-free paper.

PREFACE

These bibliographies have been compiled under the auspices of the United Methodist Studies Advisory Committee of the Division of Ordained Ministry of the General Board of Higher Education and Ministry of The United Methodist Church. They neither claim nor intend to provide exhaustive coverage of all areas of Wesleyan and Methodist scholarship. Their purpose is more modest: to provide a selected list of the basic resources for students and instructors of seminary-level courses in United Methodist history, doctrine, and polity, and to indicate minimum standards for libraries to support such courses.

In addition to standard texts, past and present, emphasis has been placed on selecting the best modern critical interpretations still in print in book form. Out of print works are included only if no suitable alternative exists in print. A few key journal articles are included in areas where there is no standard book-length treatment. Works not yet published as these bibliographies go to press are clearly indicated as "forthcoming," and are included only if there is good reason to expect their timely publication under the titles given here.

The materials in these bibliographies are arranged topically. An index of authors and editors is provided as an aid to locating works by particular individuals. The list of current periodicals published by the world-wide family of Methodist churches, given in Part 5, aims to be complete. The addresses and telephone numbers of principal suppliers of materials listed here are given in Part 8.

Corrections for items listed here and suggestions of items for inclusion in future editions of these bibliographies are welcome, and should be sent to the editor: Dr. Kenneth E. Rowe, Drew University Theological School, Madison, NJ 07940.

United Methodist Studies Advisory Committee, 1988–1992:

Richard P. Heitzenrater, *Perkins School of Theology*
Robert F. Kohler, *Division of Ordained Ministry, GBHEM*
Rex D. Matthews, *United Methodist Publishing House*
Kenneth E. Rowe, *Drew University Theological School*
Jean Miller Schmidt, *Iliff School of Theology*
Theodore H. Runyon, *Candler School of Theology*

CONTENTS

PART 1: GENERAL RESOURCES

1. Bibliographies

For specialized bibliographies, see the topical subdivisions of Part 2: History, and Part 3: Doctrine.

1001　Bowmer, John C. "Twenty-Five Years (1943–1968); I: The Work of the Wesley Historical Society; II: Methodist Studies." *Wesley Historical Society Proceedings* 37 (June 1969): 33–36; 61–66.

1002　Bucke, Emory S., ed. *History of American Methodism.* 3 vols. Nashville: Abingdon Press, 1964. See bibliographies at the end of each volume.

1003　Calkin, Homer L. *Catalog of Methodist Archival and Manuscript Collections.* [Alexandria, VA]: World Methodist Historical Society, 1982–. Part 2: Asia, 1982. Part 3: Australia and the South Pacific, 1982. Part 6: Great Britain and Ireland, 1985–91.

1004　Field, Clive D. "Bibliography of Methodist Historical Literature, 1974" (and succeeding years). Published annually in the *Wesley Historical Society Proceedings* since June 1976.

1005　———. "Bibliography." In *History of the Methodist Church in Great Britain,* 4:653–830. London: Epworth Press, 1988.

1006　———. "Preparing for the 250th: British Methodist Studies 1980–1988." *Epworth Review* 15/2 (May 1988): 95–109.

1007　———. "Sources for the Study of Protestant Nonconformity in the John Rylands University Library of Manchester." *Bulletin of the John Rylands University Library of Manchester* 71/2 (Summer 1989): [103]–139. See especially the Methodist section, 121–135.

1008　Green, Richard. *Anti-Methodist Publications Issued During the 18th Century.* New York: Burt Franklin, 1974. Reprint of the 1902 edition.

1009　Harmon, Nolan B., ed. *Encyclopedia of World Methodism.* 2 vols. Nashville: United Methodist Publishing House, 1974. See bibliographies, 2:2721–2766.

1010　John Rylands University Library of Manchester. Methodist Archives: *Catalogues, Handlists, Bibliographies and Some Important Reference Works.* 2nd edition, revised. Manchester: John Rylands University Library, 1991.

1011 Norwood, Frederick A. "Historical Study in Methodism [1988]." *Lutheran Historical Conference* 13 (1990): 173–193.

1012 ———. "Methodist Historical Studies 1930–1959." *Church History* 28 (1959): 391–417; 29 (1960): 74–88.

1013 ———. "Wesleyan and Methodist Historical Studies 1960–1970: A Bibliographical Article." *Church History* 40 (June 1971): 192–199. Reprinted in *Methodist History* 10 (January 1972): 23–44.

1014 Rack, Henry D. "Recent Books on Methodism." *Epworth Review* 7 (January 1980): 82–88.

1015 Rowe, Kenneth E. "Methodist History at the Bicentennial." *Methodist History* 22 (1984): 87–98.

1016 ———, ed. *Methodist Union Catalog, Pre–1976 Imprints*. Metuchen, NJ: Scarecrow Press. 1975–. 7 volumes (A–I) published to date.

1017 ———, ed. *The Place of Wesley in the Christian Tradition*. Revised edition. Metuchen, NJ: Scarecrow Press, 1980. Reissue of 1976 edition with updated bibliography, 134–66.

1018 Vickers, John A. *Methodism and the Wesleys*. London: World Methodist Historical Society, 1987. 50 key titles.

2. Dictionaries

1019 Crosby, Pamela J. *Speaking Connectionally (How to Speak United Methodism)*. Nashville: United Methodist Communications, 1991. A glossary of United Methodist terms, phrases, expressions and acronyms.

1020 Waltz, Alan K. *A Dictionary for United Methodists*. Nashville: Abingdon Press, 1991.

3. Directories

1021 *Directory of World Methodist Publishing*. Nashville: United Methodist Publishing House, 1991.

1022 *General Minutes of the Annual Conferences of The United Methodist Church*. Chicago: General Council on Finance and Administration, UMC, 1986. Annual statistical review, clergy lists, etc.

1023 *The United Methodist Directory and Index of Resources, 1992*. Edited by Gwen Colvin. Nashville: Cokesbury Press, 1992.

Directory of bishops, councils, boards, commissions, conferences, news services and publications, study committees, caucuses, affiliated and ecumenical groups, programs and resources. Also available from Cokesbury in electronic form.

1024　*World Methodist Council Handbook of Information 1992–1997.* Lake Junaluska, NC: World Methodist Council, 1992. Directory of executive staff, committees, member churches, international dialogues, and statistics. Published quinquennially.

4. Encyclopedias

1025　Harmon, Nolan B., ed. *Encyclopedia of World Methodism.* 2 vols. Nashville: United Methodist Publishing House, 1974.

1026　McClintock, John, and James Strong. *Cyclopedia of Biblical, Theological and Ecclesiastical Literature.* 12 vols. New York: Arno Press, 1970. Reprint of the 1867–87 edition. Still standard for the 19th century.

1027　Simpson, Matthew. *Cyclopedia of Methodism.* New York: Gordon Press, 1977. Reprint of 1878 edition. Still standard for the 19th century.

PART 2: HISTORY

1. North America

A. Surveys

2001 Bucke, Emory S., ed. *History of American Methodism.* 3 vols. Nashville: Abingdon Press, 1974.

2002 McEllhenney, John G., ed. *United Methodism in America: A Compact History.* Nashville: Abingdon Press, 1992.

2003 Norwood, Frederick A. *The Story of American Methodism: A History of the United Methodists and Their Relations.* Nashville: Abingdon Press, 1974.

2004 ———, ed. *Sourcebook of American Methodism.* Nashville: Abingdon Press, 1983.

2005 Sanderson, Joseph E. *The First Century of Methodism in Canada.* 2 vols. Toronto: William Briggs, 1908.

2006 Sweet, William W. *Methodism in American History.* Revised edition. Nashville: Abingdon Press, 1953. First published in 1933.

2007 ———. *Religion on the American Frontier, 1783–1940: The Methodists, a Collection of Source Materials.* New York: Cooper Square, 1964. Reprint of 1946 edition.

B. 18th Century Studies

2008 Andrews, Dee. *Religion and the Revolution: The Rise of the Methodists in the Middle Atlantic, 1760–1800.* Princeton: Princeton University Press, 1993. Forthcoming revision of doctoral dissertation, University of Pennsylvania, 1986.

2009 Baker, Frank. *From Wesley to Asbury: Studies in Early American Methodism.* Durham, NC: Duke University Press, 1976.

2010 Lee, Jesse. *A Short History of the Methodists.* Rutland, VT: Academy Books, 1974. Reprint of the first published history of Methodism in America, 1810.

2011 Richey, Russell E. *Early American Methodism.* Bloomington, IN: Indiana University Press, 1991.

2012 Williams, William H. *The Garden of Methodism: The Delmarva Peninsula, 1769–1820.* Wilmington, DE: Scholarly Resources Inc., 1984.

C. 19th and 20th Century Studies

2013 Jones, Donald G. *The Sectional Crisis and Northern Methodism: A Study in Piety, Political Ethics, and Civil Religion.* Metuchen, NJ: Scarecrow Press, 1979.

2014 Richey, Russell E., and Kenneth E. Rowe, eds. *Rethinking Methodist History: A Bicentennial Historical Consultation.* Nashville: Kingswood Books, 1985.

2015 Sledge, Robert Watson. *Hands on the Ark: The Struggle for Change in the Methodist Episcopal Church, South, 1914–1939.* Lake Junaluska, NC: General Commission on Archives and History, UMC, 1975.

2. Great Britain and Ireland

A. Surveys

2016 Davies, Rupert E. *Methodism.* 2nd revised edition. London: Epworth Press, 1985. Best compact survey.

2017 ——, and Gordon Rupp, eds. *A History of the Methodist Church in Great Britain.* 4 vols. London: Epworth Press, 1975–1987. The basic work on all eras.

2018 Gage, Laurie E. *English Methodism: A Bibliographical View.* Westcliff-on-Sea, Essex: Gage Postal Books, 1985.

2019 Jeffery, Frederick. *Irish Methodism: An Historical Account of its Tradition, Theology and Influences.* Belfast: Epworth House, 1964.

2020 Swift, Wesley F. *Methodism in Scotland: The First Hundred Years.* London: Epworth Press, 1947.

2021 Taggart, Norman E. *The Irish in World Methodism, 1760–1900.* London: Epworth Press, 1986.

2022 Turner, John M. *Conflict and Reconciliation: Studies in Methodism and Ecumenism in England, 1740–1982.* London: Epworth Press, 1985.

B. 18th Century Studies

For biographies of John and Charles Wesley and interpretations of their thought, see Part 3, Section 3.

2023 Baker, Frank. *John Wesley and the Church of England.* Nashville: Abingdon Press, 1970.

2024 Church Leslie F. *The Early Methodist People*. London: Epworth Press, 1948.

2025 ———. *More About the Early Methodist People*. London: Epworth Press, 1949.

2026 Heitzenrater, Richard P. *Wesley and the People Called Methodists*. Nashville: Abingdon Press, 1993? Forthcoming. The basic work on the founding era.

2027 Olsen, Gerald W., ed. *Religion and Revolution in Early Industrial England: The Halevy Thesis and its Critics*. Lanham, MD: University Press of America, 1990.

2028 Rupp, Gordon. "Evangelical Revival." In his *Religion in England 1688–1791*, 325–490. Oxford: Clarendon Press, 1986. Essential background and interpretation.

2029 Walsh, John D. "Origins of the Evangelical Revival." In *Essays in Modern English Church History*, edited by G. V. Bennett and J. D. Walsh, 132–162. New York: Oxford University Press, 1966.

C. 19th Century Studies

2030 Ambler, R. W. *Ranters, Revivalists & Reformers: Primitive Methodism and Rural Society, South Lincolnshire, 1817–1875*. Hull: Hull University Press, 1989.

2031 Carwardine, Richard. *Trans-Atlantic Revivalism: Popular Evangelicalism in Britain and America, 1790–1865*. Westport, CT: Greenwood Press, 1978.

2032 Dunlap, E. Dale. *Methodist Theology in Great Britain in the 19th Century*. Doctoral dissertation, Yale University, 1956; Ann Arbor, MI: University Microfilms International, 1968.

2033 Hempton, David. *Methodism and Politics in British Society, 1750–1850*. Stanford: Stanford University Press, 1984.

2034 Kent, John. *The Age of Disunity*. London: Epworth Press, 1966.

2035 ———. *Holding the Fort: Studies in Victorian Revivalism*. London: Epworth Press, 1978.

2036 Moore, Robert. *Pit-Men, Preachers & Politics: The Effects of Methodism in a Durham Mining Community*. Cambridge: Cambridge University Press, 1974.

2037 Semmel, Bernard. *The Methodist Revolution*. New York: Basic Books, 1973.

2038 Warner, Wellman J. *The Wesleyan Movement in the Industrial Revolution*. New York: Russell, 1967. Reprint of 1930 edition.

2039 Wearmouth, Robert F. *Methodism and the Working-Class Movements in England, 1800–1850.* Clifton, NJ: Augustus M. Kelley Publishers, 1972. Reprint of 1937 edition.

2040 Werner, Julia S. *The Primitive Methodist Connexion: Its Background and Early History.* Madison, WI: University of Wisconsin Press, 1984.

D. 20th Century Studies

2041 Brake, G. Thompson. *Policy and Politics in British Methodism, 1932–1982.* London: B. Edsall & Co., Ltd., 1985.

2042 Davies, Rupert E. *The Testing of the Churches, 1932–1982: A Symposium.* London: Epworth Press, 1982.

3. Africa

2043 Bartels, Francis L. *The Roots of Ghana Methodism.* Cambridge: Cambridge University Press, 1965.

2044 Calhoun, Eugene Clayton. *Of Men Who Ventured Much and Far: Dr. Gilbert and Bishop Lambuth.* Atlanta: The Institute Press, 1961.

2045 Cochrane, James R. *Servants of Power: The Role of English-speaking Churches in South Africa, 1903–1930; Toward a Critical Theology via an Historical Analysis of the Anglican and Methodist Churches.* Johannesburg: Ravan Press, 1987.

2046 Garrett A. E. F. *South African Methodism: Her Missionary Witness.* Cape Town, South Africa: Methodist Publishing House, 1965.

2047 Johnson, Walton R. *Worship and Freedom: A Black American Church in Zambia.* New York: Africana Publishing Co., 1977.

2048 Mears, W. Gordon. *Methodism in the Cape: An Outline.* Cape Town, South Africa: Methodist Publishing House, 1973.

2049 Muzorewa, Gwinyai H., Patrick Matsikenyiri, and Cheryl W. Reames. *Africa: Visions of Hope.* Nashville: Graded Press, 1991.

2050 Nthamburi, Rosemary K. *The Impact of the Methodist Church in Kenya in the Nineteenth Century.* Claremont, CA: Claremont Graduate School, 1978. M.A. thesis.

2051 Reid, Alexander J. *Congo Drumbeat: History of the First Half Century in the Establishment of the Methodist Church among the Atetela of Central Congo.* New York: World Outlook Press, 1964.

2052 Southon, Arthur E. *Gold Coast Methodism.* London: Cargate Press, 1934.

4. Asia and the Pacific

2053 Baker, Richard T. *Ten Thousand Years: The Story of Methodism's First Century in China.* New York: Board of Missions of The Methodist Church, 1947.

2054 Colwell, James. *The Illustrated History of Methodism: Australia, New South Wales, and Polynesia.* Sydney: W. Brooks, 1904.

2055 Deats, Richard L. *The Story of Methodism in the Philippines.* Manila: Union Theological Seminary, 1964.

2056 Grayson, James H. *Korea: A Religious History.* New York: Oxford University Press, 1989.

2057 Harper, Marvin H. *The Methodist Episcopal Church in India.* Lucknow: Lucknow Publishing House, 1936.

2058 Hollister, John N. *The Centenary of the Methodist Church in Southern Asia.* Lucknow: Lucknow Publishing House, 1956.

2059 Krummel, John W. *The Methodist Protestant Church in Japan.* 2 parts. Tokyo: Aoyama Gakuin University, 1982–1983.

2060 Lacy, Walter N. *A Hundred Years of China Methodism.* Nashville: Abingdon-Cokesbury, 1948.

2061 Walker, Alan. *Heritage Without End: A Story to Tell to the Nation.* Melbourne: Methodist Church of Australia, 1953.

5. Central and Latin America

2062 Bastian, Jean-Pierre. *Los Disidentes: Sociedades protestantes y revolución en México, 1872–1911.* México, D.F.: Fondo de Cultura Económica, Colegio de México, 1989.

2063 ——. *Protestantismo y sociedad en México.* México, D.F.: CUPSA, 1984.

2064 Díaz Acosta, Juan. *Historia de la Iglesia Evangélica Unida de Puerto Rico: Obra Evangélica para el Cincuentenario en Puerto Rico, 1899–1949.* San Juan, PR: Iglesia Evangélica Unida de Puerto Rico, 1949.

2065 Duque Zúñiga, José, ed. *La Tradición Protestante en la Teología Latinoamericana.* San José, Costa Rica: DEI, 1983. Includes essays on Methodism by Mortimer Arias, José Duque Zúñiga, José Míguez Bonino, and Elsa Tamez.

2066 *For Ever Beginning: Two Hundred Years of Methodism in the Western Area*. Kingston, Jamaica: Literature Department of the Methodist Church, Jamaica District, 1960.

2067 González, Justo L. *The Development of Christianity in the Latin Caribbean*. Grand Rapids, MI: Wm. B. Eerdmans, 1969.

2068 *Kindling of the Flame: How the Methodist Church Expanded in the Caribbean*. Demerara, British Guiana: Published for the Methodist Centenary Celebrations in the Western Area by the British Guiana District, 1960.

2069 Míguez Bonino, José, et al. *Luta pela vida e evangelização: A Tradição metodista na teologia latin-americana*. São Paulo: Ediçoes Paulinas, 1985. Essays from this volume by Mortimer Arias, Hugo Assman, Aldo Etchegoyen, and José Míguez Bonino are translated in *Faith Born in the Struggle for Life*, edited by Dow Kirkpatrick. Grand Rapids, MI: Wm. B. Eerdmans, 1988.

2070 Neblett, Sterling A. *Historia de la Iglesia Metodista en Cuba*. Buenos Aires: El Evangelista Cubano, 1973.

2071 ———. *Methodism's First Fifty Years in Cuba*. Macon GA: Wesleyan College, 1966.

2072 Pérez, Carlos. *Un Resumen de los Setenta Años de Labor de la Iglesia Metodista en Cuba, 1898–1968*. Miami: s.n., 1983.

2073 Sánchez, Gildo. *Un Jirón de Historia Metodista Unida: Testimonio de un superintendente de distrito en Puerto Rico durante su incumbencia*. San Juan, PR: s.n., 1981.

6. Europe

2074 Hagen, Odd. *Preludes to Methodism in Northern Europe*. Oslo: Norsk Forlagsselskap, 1961.

2075 Kissack, Reginald. *Methodists in Italy*. London: Cargate Press, 1960.

2076 Nauser, Wilhelm. *Be Eager to Maintain the Unity of the Spirit Through the Bond of Peace, A Short History of the Geneva Area of The United Methodist Church*. Cincinnati: General Board of Global Ministries, UMC, 1985.

2077 Short, Roy H. *History of Methodism in Europe*. Nashville: Office of the Secretary of the Council of Bishops, UMC, 1980.

2078 Stephens, Peter. *Methodism in Europe*. Cincinnati: General Board of Global Ministries, UMC, 1981.

2079 Weyer, Michel, ed. *Der kontinentaleuoropäische Methodismus zwischen den beiden Weltkriegen.* Stuttgart: Christliches Verlagshaus, 1990.

7. Biographies/Autobiographies of Principal American Figures (Men)

The General Commission on Archives and History of The United Methodist Church publishes a pamphlet biography series. Titles currently include: Jacob Albright, Richard Allen, Francis Asbury, Thomas Coke, and Philip W. Otterbein.

Albright, Jacob

2080 Miller, George. *The Life of Jacob Albright.* Translated with introduction by James D. Nelson. Dayton, OH: The Center for the Study of Evangelical United Brethren History, United Theological Seminary, 1992? Forthcoming. Albright's autobiographical reflections recorded by George Miller, first published in German in Reading, PA, in 1811.

Allen, Richard

2081 Allen, Richard. *The Life Experience and Gospel Labors of the Right Reverend Richard Allen.* Nashville: Abingdon Press, 1984. Reprint of the 1880 edition; first published in Philadelphia in 1833.

See also Part 2, Section 9: African American Methodists.

Asbury, Francis

2082 Asbury, Francis. *Journal and Letters.* Edited by Elmer T. Clark. 3 vols. Nashville: Abingdon Press, 1958.

2083 Rudolph, L. C. *Francis Asbury.* Nashville: Abingdon Press, 1983. Reprint of 1966 edition. Best biography.

Boehm, Henry

2084 Boehm, Henry. *The Patriarch of One Hundred Years, Being Reminiscences, Historical and Biographical of Rev. Henry Boehm.* Edited by J. B. Wakeley. Willow Street, PA: Boehm's Chapel Society, 1985. Reprint of 1875 edition.

Bowne, Borden Parker

2085   McConnell, Francis J. *Borden Parker Bowne: His Life and Philosophy*. New York: AMS Press, 1975. Reprint of 1929 edition.

Brownlow, William

2086   Coulter, E. Merton. *William G. Brownlow: Fighting Parson of the Southern Highlands*. Knoxville: University of Tennessee Press, 1971.

Candler, Warren

2087   Bauman, Mark K. *Warren Akin Candler: The Conservative Idealist*. Metuchen, NJ: Scarecrow Press. 1981.

Cartwright, Peter

2088   Cartwright, Peter. *Autobiography*. With introduction, bibliography and index by Charles L. Wallis. Nashville: Abingdon Press, 1986. First published in 1856.

Coke, Thomas

2089   Davey, Cyril. *Mad About Mission: The Story of Thomas Coke: Founder of the Methodist Overseas Mission*. London: Marshalls, 1985.

2090   Vickers, John A. *Thomas Coke, Apostle of Methodism*. Nashville: Abingdon Press, 1969.

Cone, James

2091   Cone, James H. *My Soul Looks Back*. Nashville: Abingdon Press, 1982.

Copway, George

2092   Copway, George. *The Life, History and Travels of Kah-Ge-Ga-Gah-Bowh (George Copway): A Young Indian Chief of the Ojebwa Nation, a Convert to the Christian Faith and a Missionary to his People for Twelve Years*. Albany, NY: Weed & Parsons, 1847.

Denman, Harry

2093   Rogers, Harold. *Harry Denman: A Biography*. Nashville: The Upper Room, 1977.

Dyer, John

2094   Fiester, Mark. *Look For Me in Heaven: The Life of John Lewis Dyer*. Boulder, CO: Pruett Publishing Co., 1980.

Finley, James

2095 Finley, James B. *Sketches of Western Methodism, Biographical, Historical, and Miscellaneous, Illustrative of Pioneer Life.* New York: Ayer Co., 1969. Reprint of 1854 edition.

Garrettson, Freeborn

2096 Garrettson, Freeborn. *American Methodist Pioneer: The Life and Journals of the Rev. Freeborn Garrettson, 1752–1827.* Edited by Robert Drew Simpson. Madison, NJ: Drew University Library, 1983.

Harmon, Nolan B.

2097 Harmon, Nolan B. *Ninety Years and Counting: Autobiography of Nolan B. Harmon.* Nashville: The Upper Room, 1983.

Haven, Gilbert

2098 Gravely, Will B. *Gilbert Haven, Methodist Abolitionist: A Study in Race, Religion and Reform, 1850–1880.* Nashville: Abingdon Press, 1973.

Hedstrom, Olaf

2099 Whyman, Henry C. *The Hedstroms and the Bethelship Saga.* Carbondale, IL: Southern Illinois University Press, 1992.

Hosier, Harry

2100 Smith, Warren T. *Harry Hosier, Circuit Rider.* Nashville: Discipleship Resources, 1981.

Inskip, John

2101 McDonald, William, and John E. Searles. *The Life of Rev. John S. Inskip.* New York: Garland Publishing, 1985. Reprint of 1885 edition.

Jones, E. Stanley

2102 Jones, E. Stanley. *A Song of Ascents: A Spiritual Autobiography.* Nashville: Abingdon Press, 1968.

Jones, Peter

2103 Smith, Donald B. *Sacred Feathers: The Rev. Peter Jones (Kah-Ke-Wa-Quo-Na-By) and the Mississauga Indians.* Lincoln: University of Nebraska Press, 1987.

Lee, Edwar

2104 Lee, Moonbeam Tong. *Growing Up in Chinatown: The Life and Work of Edwar Lee*. San Francisco: s.n., 1987.

Lee, Jason

2105 Loewenberg, Robert J. *Equality on the Oregon Frontier: Jason Lee and the Methodist Mission, 1834–1843*. Seattle: University of Washington Press, 1976.

Lee, Jesse

2106 Lee, Jesse. *Memoir of the Rev. Jesse Lee, with Extracts from his Journals*. Edited by Minton Thrift. New York: Ayer Co., 1969. Reprint of the 1823 edition.

Lee, Luther

2107 Lee, Luther. *Autobiography of the Rev. Luther Lee*. New York: Garland Publishing, 1984. Reprint of the 1882 edition.

Marksman, Peter

2108 Pitezel, John H. *The Life of Rev. Peter Marksman, an Objibwa Missionary, Illustrating the Triumphs of the Gospel among the Ojibwa Indians*. Cincinnati: Western Methodist Book Concern, 1901.

Mott, John R.

2109 Hopkins, C. Howard. *John R. Mott, 1865–1955: A Biography*. Grand Rapids, MI: Wm. B. Eerdmans Publishing Co., 1979.

Muzorewa, Abel

2110 Muzorewa, Abel T. *Rise Up and Walk: The Autobiography of Bishop Abel Tendekai Muzorewa*. Edited by Norman E. Thomas. Nashville: Abingdon Press, 1978.

North, Frank Mason

2111 Lacy, Creighton. *Frank Mason North, His Social and Ecumenical Mission*. Nashville: Abingdon Press, 1967.

Otterbein, William

2112 Core, Arthur C., ed. *Philip William Otterbein, Pastor, Ecumenist*. Dayton, OH: Board of Publication, The Evangelical United Brethren Church, 1968. Documents and commentary.

2113 O'Malley, J. Steven. *Pilgrimage of Faith: The Legacy of the Otterbeins*. Metuchen, NJ: Scarecrow Press, 1973.

Oxnam, G. Bromley

2114 Miller, Robert M. *Bishop G. Bromley Oxnam: Paladin of Liberal Protestantism*. Nashville: Abingdon Press, 1990.

Roberts, Oral

2115 Harrell, David E., Jr. *Oral Roberts: An American Life*. Bloomington, IN: Indiana University Press, 1985.

Ross, John

2116 Moulton, Gary E. *John Ross, Cherokee Chief*. Athens, GA: University of Georgia Press, 1978.

Scott, Orange

2117 Matlack, Lucius C. *The Life of Rev. Orange Scott*. New York: Ayer Co., 1971. Reprint of the 1847 edition.

Smith, A. Frank

2118 Spellman, Norman W. *Growing a Soul: The Story of A. Frank Smith*. Dallas: Southern Methodist University Press, 1979.

Strawbridge, Robert

2119 Maser, Frederick E. *Robert Strawbridge: First American Methodist Circuit Rider*. New Windsor, MD: Strawbridge Shrine Association, 1983.

Taylor, Prince

2120 Taylor Prince A., Jr. *The Life of My Years*. Nashville: Abingdon Press, 1983.

Tittle, Ernest

2121 Miller, Robert M. *How Shall They Hear Without a Preacher? The Life of Ernest Fremont Tittle*. Chapel Hill, NC: University of North Carolina Press, 1971.

Turner, Henry McNeal

2122 Angell, Stephen. *Bishop Henry McNeal Turner and African American Religion in the South*. Knoxville, TN: University of Tennessee Press, 1992

Ward, Harry

2123 Link, Eugene P. *Labor-Religion Prophet: The Times and Life of Harry F. Ward.* Boulder, CO: Westview Press, 1984.

Ware, Thomas

2124 Ware, Thomas. *Sketches of the Life and Travels of Rev. Thomas Ware, who has been an Itinerant Methodist Preacher for more than Fifty Years.* Kingsport, TN: Holston Conference Task Force on Observance of the Bicentennial of American Methodism, 1984. Reprint of the 1842 edition.

Winans, William

2125 Holder, Ray. *William Winans: Methodist Leader in Antebellum Mississippi.* University, MS: University of Mississippi Press, 1977.

White, Woodie

2126 White, Woodie W. *Confessions of a Prairie Pilgrim.* Nashville: Abingdon Press, 1988.

8. Biographies/Autobiographies of Principal American Figures (Women)

The General Commission on Archives and History of the United Methodist Church publishes a pamphlet biography series which includes Susanna Wesley, Mary Bethune and Frances Willard.

Bennett, Belle

2127 MacDonell, Mrs. Robert W. *Belle Harris Bennett: Her Life Work.* New York: Garland Publishing, 1987. Reprint of the 1928 edition.

Bethune, Mary McLeod

2128 Holt, Rackham. *Mary McLeod Bethune: A Biography.* Garden City, NY: Doubleday, 1964.

Dickey, Sarah

2129 Griffith, Helen. *Dauntless in Mississippi: The Life of Sarah Dickey, 1838–1904.* South Hadley MA: Dinosaur Press, 1966.

Elaw, Zilpha

2130 Elaw, Zilpha. "Memoirs of the Life, Religious Experience,

Ministerial Travels and Labours of Mrs. Zilpha Elaw, an American Female of Colour." In *Sisters of the Spirit*, edited by William L. Andrews, 49–160. Bloomington, IN: Indiana University Press, 1986.

Fisher, Welthy

2131 Swenson, Sally. *Welthy Honsinger Fisher, Signals of a Century: The Life and Learning of an American Educator, Literacy Pioneer and Independent Reformer in India and China.* Sittsville, Ontario: Sally Swenson, 1988.

Garrettson, Catherine

2132 Lobody, Diane. *Lost in the Ocean of Love: The Mystical Writings of Catherine Livingston Garrettson.* Bloomington, IN: Indiana University Press, 1993? Forthcoming.

Harkness, Georgia

2133 Keller, Rosemary Skinner. *Georgia Harkness: For Such a Time as This.* Nashville: Abingdon Press, 1992. Forthcoming

Henrichsen, Margaret

2134 Henrichsen, Margaret. *Seven Steeples.* New York: Harper & Row, 1953.

Lee, Jarena

2135 Lee, Jarena. "The Life and Religious Experience of Jarena Lee." In *Sisters of the Spirit*, edited by William L. Andrews, 25–48. Bloomington, IN: Indiana University Press, 1986. Excerpts from first (1836) edition of Lee's spiritual autobiography.

2136 *Spiritual Narratives: Maria W. Stewart, Jarena Lee, Julia A. Foote and Virginia W. Broughton*, with an introduction by Sue E. Houchins. New York: Oxford University Press, 1991. Contains full text of expanded (1849) edition of Lee's spiritual autobiography.

Mason, Mary

2137 North, Elizabeth Mason. *Consecrated Talents; or, The Life of Mrs. Mary W. Mason.* New York: Garland Publishing, 1987. Reprint of the 1870 edition.

Meyer, Lucy Rider

2138   Horton, Isabelle. *High Adventure: Life of Lucy Rider Meyer*. New York: Garland Publishing, 1987. Reprint of 1928 edition.

Newell, Fanny

2139   Newell, Fanny. *Memoirs of Fanny Newell, Written by Herself*. 3rd edition, with corrections and improvements. Springfield, MA: O. Scott and E. F. Newell, 1833. First published 1832.

Palmer, Phoebe

2140   Palmer, Phoebe. *Phoebe Palmer: Selected Writings*. Edited by Thomas C. Oden. New York: Paulist Press, 1988.

2141   Wheatley, Richard. *The Life and Letters of Mrs. Phoebe Palmer*. New York: Garland Publishing, 1984. Reprint of the 1876 edition.

2142   White, Charles E. *The Beauty of Holiness: Phoebe Palmer as Theologian, Revivalist, Feminist and Humanitarian*. Grand Rapids, MI: Francis Asbury Press of Zondervan Publishing House, 1986.

Shaw, Anna Howard

2143   Linkugel, Wil A., and Martha Solomon. *Anna Howard Shaw: Suffrage Orator and Social Reformer*. Westport, CT: Greenwood Press, 1990.

2144   Shaw, Anna H. *The Story of a Pioneer*. New York: Kraus Reprint Co., 1972. Reprint of the 1915 edition.

2145   ———. "My Ordination." Edited by Nancy N. Bahmueller. *Methodist History* 14/2 (January 1976): 125–131.

Smith, Amanda

2146   Smith, Amanda B. *An Autobiography: The Story of the Lord's Dealings with Mrs. Amanda Smith, the Colored Evangelist*. With an introduction by Carolyn D. Gifford. New York: Garland Publishing, 1986. Reprint of the 1893 edition.

2147   ———. *An Autobiography: The Story of the Lord's Dealings with Mrs. Amanda Smith, the Colored Evangelist*. With an introduction by Jualynne E. Dodson. New York: Oxford University Press, 1988.

Swain, Clara

2148   Swain, Clara A. *A Glimpse of India, being a Collection of Extracts from the Letters of Dr. Clara A. Swain, First Medical Missionary* to India of the Woman's Foreign Missionary Society of the Methodist Episcopal Church in America. New York: Garland Publishing, 1987. Reprint of the 1909 edition.

Willard, Frances

2149 Bordin, Ruth. *Frances Willard: A Biography*. Chapel Hill, NC: University of North Carolina Press, 1986.

2150 Willard, Frances. *Glimpses of Fifty Years: The Autobiography of an American Woman*. New York: Hacker Art Books, 1970. Reprint of the 1889 edition.

Willing, Jennie

2151 Brown, Joanne E. C. *Jennie Fowler Willing: Methodist Churchwoman and Reformer*. Doctoral dissertation, Boston University, 1983; Ann Arbor, MI: University Microfilms International, 1983.

9. African American Methodists

2152 Allen, Richard. *The Life Experiences and Gospel Labors of the Right Reverend Richard Allen*. Nashville: Abingdon Press, 1984. Reprint of the 1880 edition; first published in Philadelphia in 1833.

2153 Andrews, Dee. "The African Methodists of Philadelphia 1794–1802." *Pennsylvania Magazine of History and Biography* 108 (October 1984): 471–486.

2154 Baldwin, Lewis V. *"Invisible" Strands in African Methodism: A History of the African Union Methodist Protestant and Union American Methodist Episcopal Churches, 1805–1980*. Metuchen, NJ: Scarecrow Press, 1983.

2155 Bradley, David H. *A History of the A.M.E. Zion Church, 1796–1968*. 2 vols. Nashville: A.M.E. Zion Publishing House, 1956–1960.

2156 Culver, Dwight W. *Negro Segregation in The Methodist Church*. New Haven: Yale University Press, 1953.

2157 George Carol V. R. *Segregated Sabbaths: Richard Allen and the Rise of the Independent Black Churches, 1760–1840*. New York: Oxford University Press, 1973.

2158 Gravely, Will B. "African Methodisms and the Rise of Black Denominationalism." In *Rethinking Methodist History*, edited by Russell E. Richey and Kenneth E. Rowe, 111–124; see #2014.

2159 ——. "The Rise of African Churches in America: Re-examining the Contexts, 1786–1822." In *African American Religious Studies*, edited by G. S. Wilmore, 301–317. Durham, NC: Duke University Press, 1989.

2160 Gray C. Jarrett, Jr., comp. *The Racial and Ethnic Presence in American Methodism: A Bibliography*. Madison, NJ: General Commission on Archives and History, UMC, 1991.

2161 Gregg, Howard D. *History of the African Methodist Episcopal Church: The Black Church in Action*. Nashville: A.M.E. Church Sunday School Union, 1980.

2162 Lakey, Othal L. *The History of the C.M.E. Church*. Memphis, TN: The C.M.E. Publishing House, 1985.

2163 Lincoln, C. Eric, and Lawrence H. Mamiya. *The Black Church in the African American Experience*. Durham, NC: Duke University Press, 1990. See chapter 3.

2164 McClain, William B. *Black People in the Methodist Church: Whither Thou Goest?* Nashville: Abingdon Press, 1984.

2165 Mathews, Donald G. *Slavery and Methodism: A Chapter in American Morality, 1780–1845*. Westport, CT: Greenwood Press, 1978. Reprint of the 1965 edition.

2166 Morrow, Ralph E. *Northern Methodism and Reconstruction*. East Lansing, MI: Michigan State University Press, 1956.

2167 Murray, Peter C. *Christ and Case in Conflict: Creating a Racially Inclusive Methodist Church*. Doctoral dissertation, Indiana University, 1985; Ann Arbor, MI: University Microfilms International, 1985.

2168 Nash, Gary B. *Forging Freedom: The Formation of Philadelphia's Black Community, 1720–1840*. Cambridge: Harvard University Press, 1988. See especially chapter 4.

2169 Raboteau, Albert J., and David W. Wills. "Retelling Carter Woodson's Story: Archival Sources for Afro-American Church History." *Journal of American History* 77/1 (June 1990): 183–199.

2170 Richardson, Harry V. *Dark Salvation: The Story of Methodism as it Developed among Blacks in America*. New York: Doubleday, 1976.

2171 Shockley, Grant S., ed. *Heritage and Hope: The African American Presence in United Methodism*. Nashville: Abingdon Press, 1991. The basic work.

2172   Smith, Warren T. *Harry Hosier, Circuit Rider*. Nashville: Disci-
        pleship Resources, 1981.

2173   ——. *John Wesley and Slavery*. Nashville: Abingdon Press, 1986.
        Includes facsimile reprint of Wesley's important "Thoughts
        Upon Slavery."

2174   Thomas, James S. *Methodism's Racial Dilemma: The Story of the
        Central Jurisdiction*. Nashville: Abingdon Press, 1992.

10. Asian American Methodists

2175   Barclay, Wade C. *History of Methodist Missions*. 4 vols. New
        York: Board of Missions, The Methodist Church, 1949–
        1957. See especially 3:286–296.

2176   *The Burning Heart: Visions for Asian-American Missional Congre-
        gations*. New York: National Program Division, General
        Board of Global Ministries, UMC, 1990.

2177   Choy, Bong-Youn. *Koreans in America*. Chicago: Nelson-Hall,
        1979. See especially chapter 13, "Korean Religious and
        Cultural Activities."

2178   Gray, C. Jarrett, Jr., comp. *The Racial and Ethnic Presence in
        American Methodism: A Bibliography*. Madison, NJ: General
        Commission on Archives and History, UMC, 1991.

2179   Guillermo, Artemio R., ed. *Churches Aflame: Asian Americans
        and United Methodism*. Nashville: Abingdon Press, 1991.
        The basic work.

2180   Hurh, Wom Moo. *The Korean Immigrants in America*. Cranbury,
        NJ: Associated University Press, 1984.

2181   Kim, Byong-suh, and Sang Hyun Lee, eds. *The Korean Immi-
        grant in America*. New Jersey: Association of Korean Chris-
        tian Scholars in North America, 1980.

2182   Kim, Hyung-chan. *The Korean Diaspora*. Santa Rosa, CA: Clio
        Publications, 1977. Especially "History and Role of the
        Church in the Korean American Community," 47–64.

2183   Kim, Illsoo. *New Urban Immigrants: The Korean Community in
        New York*. Princeton, NJ: Princeton University Press, 1981.
        Includes major section on the churches.

2184   ——. "Organizational Patterns of Korean-American Methodist
        Churches: Denominationalism and Personal Community."
        In *Rethinking Methodist History*, edited by Russell E. Richey
        and Kenneth E. Rowe, 228–238; see #2014.

27

2185 Koga, Sumio, comp. *A Centennial Legacy: History of the Japanese Christian Missions in North America.* Chicago: Nobart Inc., 1977.

2186 National Federation of Asian American United Methodists. *Retrospection & Projection.* 5 vols. San Francisco: The Federation, 1981–1985.

2187 Suzuki, Lester E. *Ministry in the Assembly and Relocation Centers of World War II.* Berkeley, CA: Yardbird Publishing Co., 1979.

2188 Woo, Wesley S. *Protestant Work Among the Chinese in the San Francisco Bay Area, 1850–1920.* Doctoral dissertation, Graduate Theological Union, 1984; Ann Arbor, MI: University Microfilms International, 1984.

11. Chaplains

2189 Boozer, Jack S. *Edge of Ministry–The Chaplain Story: The Chaplain Ministry of The United Methodist Church, 1945–1980.* Nashville: General Board of Higher Education and Ministry, UMC, 1984.

12. Charismatic Methodists

2190 Bartelman, Frank. *Azuza Street, 1907.* South Plainfield, NJ: Bridge Publications, 1980.

2191 Davison, Leslie. *Pathway to Power: The Charismatic Movement in Historical Perspective.* Watchung, NJ: Logos Books, 1972.

2192 Dayton, Donald W. *The Theological Roots of Pentecostalism.* Grand Rapids, MI: Francis Asbury Press of Zondervan Publishing House, 1987.

2193 Greet, Kenneth. *When the Spirit Moves.* London: Epworth Press, 1975.

2194 *Guidelines: The United Methodist Church and the Charismatic Renewal.* Nashville: Discipleship Resources, 1976. A statement approved by the 1976 General Conference.

2195 Jones, Charles E. *A Guide to the Study of the Pentecostal Movement.* 2 vols. Metuchen, NJ: Scarecrow Press, 1983.

2196 ——. *The Charismatic Movement: A Guide to the Study of Neo-Pentecostalism, with Emphasis on Anglo-American Sources.* Metuchen, NJ: Scarecrow Press, 1992.

2197 McDonnell, Kilian, ed. *Presence, Power, Praise: Documents on the*

Charismatic Renewal. 3 vols. Collegeville, MN: Liturgical Press, 1980. Contains full texts of the official resolutions and study documents of Methodist Churches in Australia, England, and the United States.

2198 Snyder, Howard A., with Daniel V. Runyon. *The Divided Flame: Wesleyans and the Charismatic Renewal.* Grand Rapids, MI: Francis Asbury Press of Zondervan Publishing House, 1986.

2199 Stokes, Mack B. *The Holy Spirit in the Wesleyan Heritage.* Nashville: Graded Press, 1985.

2200 Tuttle, Robert G., Jr. "Can United Methodists Be Charismatics?" *Circuit Rider* 2/6 (April 1978): 3–6.

2201 Wesley, John. "Cautions and Directions Given to the Greatest Professors in the Methodist Societies" (1762). In *John Wesley,* edited by Albert C. Outler, 298–305; see #3036.

2202 ———. "The Nature of Enthusiasm" (1750). Sermon 37 in *The Works of John Wesley* (Bicentennial Edition), 2:44–60.

2203 ———. "The Witness of the Spirit, Discourses I and II" (1746 and 1767). Sermons 10–11 in *The Works of John Wesley* (Bicentennial Edition), 1:267–298.

13. Christian Education

2204 Bowen, Cawthon A. *Child and Church: A History of Methodist Church School Curriculum.* New York: Abingdon, 1960.

2205 *Foundations for Teaching and Learning in The United Methodist Church: A Statement of the Division of Education, Board of Discipleship, The United Methodist Church.* Nashville: Discipleship Resources, 1979. Also study guide and learning kit. Available in Spanish and Korean.

2206 Hartman, Warren J. *A Look at Some Excellent Church Schools.* Nashville: Discipleship Resources, 1977.

2207 Price, Elizabeth B., and Charles R. Foster. *By What Authority? A Conversation on Teaching Among United Methodists.* Nashville: Abingdon Press, 1991.

2208 Ryan, Roy H., ed. *Christian Education Planning Handbook for the Sunday School and Other Educational Opportunities.* Nashville: Discipleship Resources, 1988.

2209 Schisler, John Q. *Christian Education in Local Methodist Churches.* Nashville: Abingdon Press, 1969. The basic history.

2210　Shockley, Grant S., and Ethel R. Johnson. *The Christian Education Journey of Black Americans*. Nashville: Discipleship Resources, 1985.

14. Church Architecture

2211　Dolby, George W. *The Architectural Expression of Methodism: The First Hundred Years*. London: Epworth Press, 1964. Discusses England only.

2212　Garber, Paul Neff. *The Methodist Meeting House*. New York: Board of Missions and Church Extension, The Methodist Church, 1941.

2213　Jaeger, A. Robert. *The Auditorium and Akron Plans: Reflections on a Half Century of American Protestantism*. M.A. thesis, Cornell University, 1984.

2214　White, James F. "Early Methodist Liturgical Architecture." *Motive* 18 (1958): 12–13, 19–20.

2215　———. *Protestant Worship and Church Architecture: Theological and Historical Considerations*. New York: Oxford University Press, 1964.

2216　———. "Theology and Architecture in America: A Study of Three Leaders." In *A Miscellany of American Christianity: Essays in Honor of H. Shelton Smith*, edited by Stuart C. Henry, 362–390. Durham, NC: Duke University Press, 1963.

2217　———, and Susan J. White. *Church Architecture: Building and Renovating for Christian Worship*. Nashville: Abingdon Press, 1988.

15. Class Meeting

See also Part 2, Section 32: Spirituality.

2218　Holsclaw, David F. *The Decline of Disciplined Christian Fellowship: The Methodist Class Meeting in Nineteenth-Century America*. Doctoral dissertation, University of California, Davis, 1979; Ann Arbor MI: University Microfilms International, 1979.

2219　Littell, Franklin H. "The Methodist Class Meeting as an Instrument of Christian Discipline." *World Parish* 9/1 (February 1961): 14–24.

2220 Watson, David L. *Class Leaders: Recovering a Tradition*. Nashville: Discipleship Resources, 1991.

2221 ———. *Covenant Discipleship: Christian Formation Through Mutual Accountability*. Nashville: Discipleship Resources, 1991. The basic program guide, designed to be used with *Class Leaders* and *Forming Christian Disciples*.

2222 ———. *The Early Methodist Class Meeting: Its Origins and Significance*. Nashville: Discipleship Resources, 1985. The basic historical work.

2223 ———. *Forming Christian Disciples: The Role of Covenant Discipleship and Class Leaders in the Congregation*. Nashville: Discipleship Resources, 1991.

2224 Wesley, John. "The Nature, Design, and General Rules of the United Societies" (1743). In *The Works of John Wesley* (Bicentennial Edition), 9:67–75. See also "Rules and Directions to the Band Societies," 9:77–79. Both texts also in *John Wesley*, edited by Albert C. Outler, 177–81; see #3033. Cf. "The General Rules of the Methodist Church," *The Book of Discipline*, 1988, 74–77 (¶68).

2225 ———. "A Plain Account of the People Called Methodists" (1748). In *The Works of John Wesley* (Bicentennial Edition), 9:253–280.

16. Ecumenism

A. Surveys

2226 Lyles, Jean Caffey. *A Practical Vision of Christian Unity*. Nashville: Abingdon Press, 1982.

2227 Minus, Paul M., ed. *Methodism's Destiny in an Ecumenical Age*. New York: Abingdon Press, 1969.

2228 Outler, Albert C. *That the World May Believe: A Study of Christian Unity and What It Means for Methodists*. New York: Board of Missions, The Methodist Church, 1966.

2229 Richey, Russell E., ed. *Ecumenical and Interreligious Perspective: Globalization in Theological Education*. Nashville: General Board of Higher Education and Ministry, UMC, 1992. Papers delivered at the Yahara Consultation of Methodist Theological Educators, March 1990.

2230 Wainwright, Geoffrey. *The Ecumenical Moment: Crisis and*

Opportunity for the Church. Grand Rapids, MI: Wm. B. Eerdmans, 1983.

2231 Washburn, Paul. *An Unfinished Church: A Brief History of the Union of the Evangelical United Brethren Church and the Methodist Church.* Nashville: Abingdon Press, 1985.

B. The Ecumenical Wesley

2232 Wesley, John. "The Catholic Spirit" (1750). Sermon 39 in *The Works of John Wesley* (Bicentennial Edition), 2:81–95.

2233 ——. "Letter to a Roman Catholic" (1749). In *John Wesley,* edited by Albert C. Outler, 493–499; see #3036. For annotated edition, see *John Wesley's Letter to a Roman Catholic,* edited by Michael Hurley. Nashville: Abingdon Press, 1968.

2234 ——. "On Schism" (1786). Sermon 75 in *The Works of John Wesley* (Bicentennial Edition), 3:58–69.

C. The Ecumenical Asbury

2235 Asbury, Francis, ed. *The Causes, Evils, and Cures of Heart and Church Divisions.* Salem, Ohio: Schmul Publishers, 1978. Asbury's selections from Richard Baxter and Jeremiah Burroughs. Reprint of the 1856 edition; first published in 1792.

D. Official UMC Resolutions

The individual resolutions cited below can be found in *The Book of Resolutions of The United Methodist Church,* 1992.

2236 "Act of Covenanting between other Christian Churches and The United Methodist Church," 1988.

2237 "Affirmation of Membership in the World and National Councils of Churches and in the Consultation on Church Union," 1992.

2238 "COCU Consensus: In Quest of a Church of Christian Uniting," 1988.

2239 "Ecumenical Interpretation of Doctrinal Standards," 1970, reaffirmed 1992.

2240 "Guidelines for Interreligious Relationships: 'Called to be Neighbors and Witnesses,'" 1980.

2241 "Mutual Recognition of Members," 1984.

2242   "On the Ecumenical Road: The United Methodist Church and the Cause of Christian Unity," 1968. Also available in pamphlet form from GCCUIC. The basic resolution.

2243   *Christian Unity: Imperatives and New Commitments.* New York: General Commission on Christian Unity and Interreligious Concerns, 1978. Basic statement by the Council of Bishops of The United Methodist Church.

E. Christian-Muslim Dialogue

2244   "Our Muslim Neighbors," 1992. In *Book of Resolutions, 1992.*

F. Commission on Pan-Methodist Cooperation

2245   Consultation of Methodist Bishops. *Proceedings.* Edited 1979–1991 by C. Faith Richardson; edited 1991– by Mary A. Love. 5 vols. Washington, DC and Charlotte, NC: Secretary of the Consultation, 1979– . Reports of the first five meetings (lst 1979, 2nd 1981, 3rd 1983, 4th 1987, 5th 1991) of the first bishops of the A.M.E. Church, the A.M.E. Zion Church, the Christian Methodist Episcopal Church, and the United Methodist Church to map strategy for joint action and future unity.

G. Consultation on Church Union (COCU)

2246   Consultation on Church Union. *Churches in Covenant Communion.* Princeton, NJ: COCU, 1989. Proposed plan of church unity in which member churches accept eight "elements" which include a common apostolic faith, recognition of members in one baptism, and mutual recognition and reconciliation of the ordained ministry. Member churches would retain their own denominational names, identity, church governments, liturgy, and patterns of ministerial training and placement.

2247   ——. *COCU Consensus: In Quest of a Church of Christ Uniting.* Princeton, NJ: COCU, 1985. Doctrinal agreement by nine parent denominations on what constitutes the core of the apostolic faith.

2248   Moede, Gerald F. *Oneness in Christ: The Quest and the Question.* Princeton, NJ: COCU, 1981.

2249   ——. *Toward Unity in Covenant Communion.* Princeton, NJ: COCU, 1988.

2250 Nelson, J. Robert. "The Critics and the Nature of the Unity We Seek." In *Church Union At Midpoint*, edited by Paul A. Crow and William J. Boney, 141–155. New York: Association Press, 1972.

H. Jewish/Christian Dialogue

2251 *Jewish-Christian Dialogue: Bridge in Hope*. Cincinnati: Service Center, General Board of Global Ministries, UMC, 1972. Statement adopted by the 1972 General Conference.

I. Methodist/Lutheran International Dialogue

Joint Commission between the Lutheran World Federation and the World Methodist Council, 1979–1984:

2252 "The Church: Community of Grace." Final report 1979–1984 in World Methodist Conference (15th: Nairobi, 1986) *Proceedings*, 342–360. Lake Junaluska, NC: World Methodist Council, 1987.

2253 *Vom Dialog zur Kanzel- und Abendmahlsgemeinschaft; eine Dokumentation der Lehrgespräche und der Beschlüsse der kirchenleitenden Gemeinde*. Herausgegeben vom Lutherischen und Evangelisch-Methodistischen Kirche. Hannover: Lutherisches Verlagshaus; Stuttgart: Christliches Verlagshaus, 1987.

J. Methodist/Orthodox Dialogue

2254 Frost, Brian. *Living in Tension Between East and West*. London: New World Publications, 1984.

2255 Maddox, Randy L. "John Wesley and Eastern Orthodoxy." *Asbury Theological Journal* 45/2 (Fall 1990): 29-53.

K. Methodist/Reformed International Dialogue

International Consultation between the World Alliance of Reformed Churches and the World Methodist Council:

1st, London Colney, England, 1985:

2256 "Our Common Faith." In World Methodist Conference (15th: Nairobi, 1986) *Proceedings*, 339–342. Lake Junaluska, NC: World Methodist Council, 1987.

2257 Marshall, I. Howard. *Kept by the Power of God: A Study of Perseverance and Falling Away*. London: Epworth, 1969.

2258 Sell, Alan P. F. *The Great Debate: Calvinism, Arminianism and Salvation.* Grand Rapids, MI: Baker Book House, 1983.

2259 "Together in God's Grace." *Reformed World* 39/8 (December 1987): 823–28.

2260 Wainwright, Geoffrey. *Geoffrey Wainwright on Wesley and Calvin: Sources for Theology, Liturgy and Spirituality.* Melbourne: Uniting Church Press, 1987.

2261 ———. "Perfect Salvation in the Teaching of Wesley and Calvin." *Reformed World* 40/2 (June 1988): 898–909.

L. Methodist/Roman Catholic International Dialogue

Joint Commission between the Roman Catholic Church
and the World Methodist Council:

1st series, 1967–1970:

2262 Denver Report, in World Methodist Conference (12th: Denver, 1971) *Proceedings*, 39–68. Nashville: Abingdon Press, 1972.

2nd series, 1972–1975:

2263 Dublin Report, in World Methodist Conference (13th: Dublin, 1976) *Proceedings*, 254–270. Lake Junaluska, NC: World Methodist Council, 1977.

3rd series, 1977–1981:

2264 Honolulu Report, in World Methodist Conference (14th: Honolulu, 1981) *Proceedings*, 264–277. Lake Junaluska, NC: World Methodist Council, 1982.

2265 Reports 1–3 are conveniently found in: *Growth in Agreement: Reports and Agreed Statements of Ecumenical Conversations on a World Level*, edited by Harding Meyer and Lukas Vischer, 307–387. Mahwah, NJ: Paulist Press, 1984.

4th series, 1981–1986:

2266 Nairobi Report. "Towards a Statement on the Church" in World Methodist Conference (15th: Nairobi, 1986) *Proceedings*, 360–372. Lake Junaluska, NC: World Methodist Council, 1987.

5th series, 1986–1991:

2267 Singapore Report. *The Apostolic Tradition.* Lake Junaluska, NC:

World Methodist Council, 1991. Also in World Methodist Conference (16th: Singapore, 1991) *Proceedings*. Lake Junaluska, NC: World Methodist Council, 1992. Check index.

General Studies:

2268 Massa, Mark S. "The Catholic Wesley: A Revisionist Prolegomenon." *Methodist History* 22 (1983–84): 38–53.

2269 *One in Christ* 22 (1986). See articles by C. Rand, G. Tavard & G. Wainwright and the Nairobi Report with commentary by J.-M. R. Tillard.

2270 Outler, Albert C. "An Olive Branch to the Romans, 1970s Style: United Methodist Initiative, Roman Catholic Response." *Methodist History* 13 (January 1975): 52–56. Includes full text of the 1970 General Conference "Resolution of Intent" to interpret the Articles of Religion of the UMC in the light of current ecumenical commitments, plus background, commentary and official Roman Catholic response.

2271 Wainwright, Geoffrey. *The Ecumenical Moment.* Grand Rapids, MI: Wm. B. Eerdmans, 1983. See especially chapters 10–11.

M. United Methodist/Lutheran Dialogue (US)

1st series, 1977- 1979:

2272 "A Lutheran-United Methodist Statement on Baptism." *Perkins Journal* 34/2 (1981): 1–56.

2nd series, 1985–1988:

2273 *Episcopacy: A Lutheran/United Methodist Common Statement to the Church.* Cincinnati: Service Center, General Board of Global Ministries, UMC, 1987. Preliminary report.

2274 *Episcopacy: Lutheran/United Methodist Dialogue II.* Edited by Jack M. Tuell and Roger W. Fjeld. Minneapolis: Augsburg, 1991. Final report.

N. United Methodist/Roman Catholic Dialogue (US)

1st series, 1966–1970:

"Shared Convictions about Education, 1970"; see #2277.

2nd series, 1971–1976:

2275 *Holiness and Spirituality of the Ordained Ministry.* Washington:

Publication Office, United States Catholic Conference, 1976. Also in *Ecumenical Trends* 5/3 (March, 1976): 33–45.

3rd series, 1977–1981:

2276 *Eucharistic Celebration: Converging Theology–Divergent Practice.* Cincinnati: Service Center, General Board of Global Ministries, UMC, 1981.

2277 The first three UM/RC USA reports may be found in *Building Unity: Ecumenical Dialogues with Roman Catholic Participation in the United States,* edited by Joseph A. Burgess and Jeffrey Gros, 291–322. New York: Paulist Press, 1989.

4th series, 1986–1989:

2278 *Holy Living, Holy Dying: A United Methodist/Roman Catholic Common Statement.* Cincinnati: Service Center, General Board of Global Ministries, UMC, 1989.

2279 "Understanding Living and Dying as Faithful Christians." 1992 resolution. In *Book of Resolutions, 1992.*

General Study:

2280 Russalesi, Steven D. *The History of Roman Catholic-United Methodist Dialogue in the United States, 1966–1989: A Theological Appraisal.* Doctoral dissertation, Catholic University of America, 1991; Ann Arbor, University Microfilms International, 1992.

O. World Council of Churches

2281 *Baptism, Eucharist and Ministry.* Faith & Order Paper No. 111. Geneva: World Council of Churches, 1982.

2282 *Churches Respond to BEM: Official Responses to the "Baptism, Eucharist and Ministry" Text,* Vol. 2. Edited by Max Thurian. Geneva: World Council of Churches, 1986. See United Methodist Church (USA), 177–199; United Methodist Church (Central and Southern Europe), 200–209; Methodist Church (UK), 210–229; Methodist Church in Ireland, 230–235; Methodist Church of South Africa, 236–244; Waldensian and Methodist Churches in Italy, 245–254.

2283 Deschner, John. "The Changing Shape of the Church Unity Question." In *Faith and Order 1985–1989: The Commission Meeting at Budapest, 1989,* edited by Thomas F. Best, 44–54. Faith & Order Paper No. 148. Geneva: World Council of Churches, 1990.

2284 ———. "The Unity of the Church and the Renewal of the Human Community." In *Towards Visible Unity: Commission on Faith and Order, 1982,* edited by Michael Kinnamon, 184–197. Faith & Order Paper No. 113. Geneva: World Council of Churches, 1982.

2285 *Interdenominational Cooperation Fund: Together in Faith.* Nashville: United Methodist Communications, 1988.

17. Ethnicity

See also separate sections on African, Asian, Hispanic, and Native American Methodists.

2286 Andersen, Arlo W. *The Salt of the Earth: A History of Norwegian-Danish Methodism in America.* Nashville: Parthenon Press, 1962.

2287 Douglass, Paul F. *The Story of German Methodism: Biography of an Immigrant Soul.* New York: Methodist Book Concern, 1939.

2288 González, Justo L. *Out of Every Tribe and Nation: Christian Theology at the Ethnic Roundtable.* Nashville: Abingdon Press, 1992.

2289 Mangano, Antonio. *Religious Work among Italians in America: A Survey for the Home Missions Council.* Philadelphia: Board of Home Missions and Church Extension of the Methodist Episcopal Church, [1917].

2290 Sano, Roy I. *From Every Nation Without Number: Racial and Ethnic Diversity in United Methodism.* Nashville: Abingdon Press, 1982.

2291 Wimberly, Anne S. *Language of Hospitality: Intercultural Relations in the Household of God.* Nashville: Cokesbury Press, 1991. An official resource prepared by the General Board of Discipleship through the Division of Church School Publications.

2292 Whyman Henry C. *The History of Ethnic Ministries in the New York Conference, The United Methodist Church.* New York: New York Conference Bicentennial Committee, 1984.

2293 *Words that Hurt and Words that Heal: Language about God and People.* New edition. Nashville: Graded Press, 1991. Leader's guide plus full text of document prepared in 1988 by the United Methodist Task Force on Language Guidelines.

18. Evangelical and United Brethren Traditions

2294 Behney, J. Bruce, and Paul H. Eller. *The History of the Evangelical United Brethren Church.* Nashville: Abingdon Press, 1979.

2295 Longenecker, Stephen L. *Democracy's Pulpit: Religion and Egalitarianism among early Pennsylvania Germans.* Doctoral dissertation, Johns Hopkins University, 1990; Ann Arbor, MI: University Microfilms International, 1990. See especially chapter 5, "Wachet auf: The Pennsylvania German Awakening," and chapter 6, "The New Revivalists."

19. Evangelical Methodists

2296 Keysor, Charles W. "Methodism's Silent Minority: A Voice for Orthodoxy." *Christian Advocate* 10 (July 14, 1966): 9–10. Founding article for the Good News movement.

2297 ———. "The Story of Good News." *Good News* 14 (March-April 1981). Special issue.

2298 McCutcheon, William J., and William Neill. "United Methodist Evangelicals in Two Generations: The 1920s and the 1930s." *Explor* 2/2 (Fall 1976): 59–72.

20. Evangelism

See also Part 2, Section 15: Class Meeting.

2299 Arias, Mortimer. *Announcing the Reign of God: Evangelization and the Subversive Message of Jesus.* Philadelphia: Fortress Press, 1984.

2300 ———, and Alan Johnson. *The Great Commission: Biblical Models for Evangelism.* Nashville: Abingdon Press, 1992.

2301 Harding, Joe A., and Ralph W. Mohney. *Vision 2000: Planning for Ministry into the Next Century.* Nashville: Discipleship Resources, 1991.

2302 Outler, Albert C. *Evangelism in the Wesleyan Spirit.* Nashville: Discipleship Resources, 1971.

2303 Tuttle, Robert G., Jr. *On Giant Shoulders: The History, Role and Influence of the Evangelist in the Movement called Methodism.* Nashville: Discipleship Resources, 1984.

2304 United Methodist Church, Council of Bishops. *Vital Congregations/Faithful Disciples: Vision for the Church.* Nashville:

Graded Press, 1990. Pastoral Letter, foundation document, leader's guide, and video.

2305 Wilke, Richard B. *And Are We Yet Alive? The Future of The United Methodist Church.* Nashville: Abingdon Press, 1986.

2306 Willimon, William H., and Robert L. Wilson. *Rekindling the Flame: Strategies for a Vital United Methodism.* Nashville: Abingdon Press, 1987.

21. Healing and Health Care

2307 Crouch, Timothy J., ed. and comp. *A United Methodist Rite for Anointing.* Cleveland: Order of St. Luke Publications, 1986.

2308 Crummey, David C. *Factors in the Rise of Methodist Hospitals and Homes.* Doctoral dissertation, University of Chicago, 1963.

2309 Day, Albert E. *Letters on the Healing Ministry,* with study guide by James K. Wagner. Nashville: The Upper Room, 1986. Reprint of 1946 edition.

2310 Hill, A. Wesley. *John Wesley Among the Physicians: A Study of 18th-Century Medicine.* London: Epworth Press, 1958.

2311 Holifield, E. Brooks. *Health and Medicine in the Methodist Tradition.* New York: Crossroads/Continuum, 1986.

2312 Wagner, James K. *Blessed to be a Blessing: How to Have an Intentional Healing Ministry in Your Church.* Nashville: The Upper Room, 1980.

2313 Wesley, John. "On Visiting the Sick" (1786). Sermon 98 in *The Works of John Wesley* (Bicentennial Edition), 3:384–397.

2314 ———. *Primitive Remedies.* Santa Barbara, CA: Woodbridge Press Publishing Co., 1973. Reprint of 1755 edition.

2315 ———. *Wesley's Primitive Physick.* Library of Methodist Classics. Nashville: United Methodist Publishing House, 1992. Facsimile reprint of the first printing by the Methodists in America, 1791.

22. Higher Education

For works on Theological Education, see Part 3, Section 9.

2316 Baker, James C. *The First Wesley Foundation: An Adventure in Christian Higher Education.* Nashville: Parthenon, 1960.

2317 Bowser, Beth A. *A History of the University Senate in the Methodist Episcopal Church, The Methodist Church, and The United*

Methodist Church. Doctoral dissertation, University of Akron, 1990; Ann Arbor, MI: University Microfilms International 1990.

2318 Cole, Charles E., ed. *Something More Than Human: Biographies of Leaders in American Methodist Higher Education.* Nashville: General Board of Higher Education and Ministry, UMC, 1986.

2319 Conn, Robert A. *Handbook for Higher Education and Campus Ministry in the Annual Conference.* Nashville: General Board of Higher Education and Ministry, UMC, 1989.

2320 Dent, Frank Lloyd. *"Motive" Magazine: Advocating the Arts and Empowering the Imagination in the Life of the Church.* Doctoral dissertation, Columbia University, 1989; Ann Arbor, MI: University Microfilms International, 1989.

2321 Duvall, Sylvanus M. *The Methodist Episcopal Church and Education up to 1869.* New York: Bureau of Publications, Teacher's College, Columbia University, 1928.

2322 Hauenstein-Mallett, Kim A., and Kenda C. Dean. *Covenants on Campus: Covenant Discipleship Groups for College and University Students.* Nashville: Discipleship Resources, 1991.

2323 Johnson, Terrell E. *A History of Methodist Education and its Influence on American Public Education.* Doctoral dissertation, Southern Illinois University at Carbondale, 1989; Ann Arbor, MI: University Microfilms International, 1989.

23. Hispanic American Methodists

2324 González, Justo L., ed. *Each in Our Own Tongue: A History of Hispanic United Methodism.* Nashville: Abingdon Press, 1991. Also available in Spanish: *En nuestra propria lengua.* The basic work.

2325 ——, ed. *Voces: Voices from the Hispanic Church.* Nashville: Abingdon Press, 1992.

2326 Gray, C. Jarrett, Jr., comp. *The Racial and Ethnic Presence in American Methodism: A Bibliography.* Madison, NJ: General Commission on Archives and History, UMC, 1991.

2327 Harwood, Thomas. *History of the New Mexico, Spanish and English Missions of the Methodist Episcopal Church from 1850 to 1910.* 2 vols. Albuquerque, NM: El Abogado Press, 1908–1910.

2328　*The Hispanic Vision for Century III.* San Antonio, TX: MARCHA, the National Hispanic United Methodist Caucus, 1985.

2329　Náñez, Alfredo. *Historia de la Conferencia Río Grande de la Iglesia Metodista Unida.* Dallas: Bridwell Library, Southern Methodist University, 1981. Also available in English.

2330　UMC Study Committee on Hispanic Ministries. "Report to the 1992 General Conference." *Daily Christian Advocate* (1992 advance edition). For the background of and rationale for the Committee's report, see "Hispanic Ministries: Challenge and Opportunity" (1992), available from GCOM.

24. Holiness Movement

Includes the Church of the Nazarene, Free Methodist, Primitive Methodist, and Wesleyan Methodist traditions in the US. See also Part 2, Section 19: Evangelical Methodists, and Part 3, Section 6: History of Doctrine.

2331　Acornley, John H. *A History of the Primitive Methodist Church in the United States of America.* Fall River, MA: N.W. Matthews, 1909.

2332　Caldwell, Wayne E., ed. *Reformers and Revivalists.* Wesleyan History series, Vol. 3. Indianapolis: Wesley Press, 1992.

2333　Dayton, Donald W. *Discovering an Evangelical Heritage.* Peabody, MA: Hendrickson Publishers, 1988. Reprint of the 1976 edition.

2334　——. *The Theological Roots of Pentecostalism.* Metuchen, NJ: Scarecrow Press, 1987.

2335　Dieter, Melvin E. *The Holiness Revival of the Nineteenth Century.* Metuchen, NJ: Scarecrow Press, 1980.

2336　Jones, Charles E. *A Guide to the Study of the Holiness Movement.* Metuchen, NJ: Scarecrow Press, 1974.

2337　——. *Perfectionist Persuasion: The Holiness Movement and American Methodism, 1867–1936.* Metuchen, NJ: Scarecrow Press, 1974.

2338　McLeister, Ira Ford. *Conscience and Commitment: The History of the Wesleyan Methodist Church of America.* 4th revised edition. Wesleyan History series, Vol. 1. Marion, IN: Wesley Press, 1976.

2339 Marston, Leslie Ray. *From Age to Age A Living Witness: A Historical Interpretation of Free Methodism's First Hundred Years*. Winona Lake, IN: Light and Life Press, 1960.

2340 Miller, William C. *Holiness Works: A Bibliography*. Revised edition. Kansas City, MO: Beacon Hill Press, 1986.

2341 Smith, Timothy L. *Called Unto Holiness: The Story of the Nazarenes, the Formative Years*. Kansas City: Nazarene Publishing House, 1962.

2342 ———. "The Holiness Crusade." In *History of American Methodism*, edited by Emory S. Bucke, 2:608–627; see #2001.

2343 ———. *Revivalism and Social Reform: American Protestantism on the Eve of the Civil War*. New York: Peter Smith, 1976. Reprint of 1957 edition.

2344 Sweet, Leonard I., ed. *The Evangelical Tradition in America*. Macon, GA: Mercer University Press, 1984.

2345 Synan, Vinson. *The Holiness-Pentecostal Movement*. Grand Rapids, MI: Wm. B. Eerdmans, 1972.

2346 Thomas, Paul W. *The Days of our Pilgrimage: The History of the Pilgrim Holiness Church*. Wesleyan History series, Vol. 2. Marion, IN: Wesley Press, 1976.

2347 Walls, Francine E. *The Free Methodist Church: A Bibliography*. Winona Lake, IN: Free Methodist Historical Center, 1977.

25. Human Sexuality

2348 Abelove, Henry. *The Evangelist of Desire: John Wesley and the Methodists*. Stanford, CA: Stanford University Press, 1990. See chapter 5, "Sexuality."

2349 Babuscio, Jack. *We Speak for Ourselves: The Experiences of Gay Men and Lesbians*. Nashville: Abingdon Press, 1991.

2350 Blair, Ralph. *Wesleyan Praxis and Homosexual Practice*. New York: HCCC, Inc., 1983. Address delivered at the Michigan Area UMC Pastor's School, August, 1983.

2351 Boyd, Malcolm, ed. *Amazing Grace: Stories of Gay and Lesbian Faith*. Freedom, CA: Crossing Press, 1991.

2352 Cook, Ann Thompson. *And God Loves Each One: A Resource for Dialogue about the Church and Homosexuality*. Washington, DC: Task Force on Reconciliation, Dumbarton United Methodist Church, 1988.

2353 Furnish, Victor P., et al. *Homosexuality in Search of a Christian Understanding: Biblical, Theological-Ethical and Pastoral Care Perspectives.* Nashville: Discipleship Resources, 1981.

2354 Hilton, Bruce. *Can Homophobia be Cured? Wrestling with Questions that Challenge the Church.* Nashville: Abingdon Press, 1992.

2355 Koehler, George E. *Guide to the Study Document on Human Sexuality.* Nashville: Discipleship Resources, 1983. Includes the full text of the 1980 General Conference "Study Document on Human Sexuality."

2356 Mace, David. *The Christian Response to the Sexual Revolution.* Updated edition. Nashville: Abingdon Press, 1987.

2357 Methodist Church (Great Britain) Commission on Human Sexuality. *Human Sexuality: A Study Guide to the report presented to the Methodist Conference 1990.* London: Methodist Publishing House, 1991.

2358 Meyers, Patricia A. *Here is My Hand: A Study Guide on Being Reconciled with all God's Children.* Portland, OR: United Methodist Conference Center, 1991.

2359 Mickey, Paul A. *Of Sacred Worth.* Nashville: Abingdon Press, 1991.

2360 "Our History: Affirmation Time-Line." *Affirmation Newsletter* (Summer 1989): 1, 3–4.

2361 Switzer, David K., and Shirley Switzer. *Parents of the Homosexual.* Philadelphia: Westminster Press, 1980.

2362 *Thinking It Through: United Methodists Look at the Church and Homosexuality.* Revised edition. Staten Island, NY: Methodist Federation for Social Action, 1990. Comprehensive study packet.

2363 "Timeline: 25 Years of the Lesbian/Gay Christian Movement." *Open Hands* 5/3 (Winter 1990): 10–13.

2364 UMC Committee to Study Homosexuality. "Report to the 1992 General Conference." *Daily Christian Advocate* (1992 advance edition).

26. Hymnology

A. Collections of Hymns

2365   Allen, Richard. *A Collection of Hymns and Spiritual Songs*. Nashville: African Methodist Episcopal Church Sunday School Union, 1987. Reprint of 1801 edition.

2366   *Celebremos, segunda parte: Cóleccion de Himnos, Salmos y Cánticos*. Edited by Roberto Escamilla. Nashville: Discipleship Resources, 1983.

2367   *Cokesbury Worship Hymnal*. Nashville: Abingdon Press, 1988. First published in 1938.

2368   *Himnario Metodista*. Nashville: Casa de publicaciones de La Iglesia Metodista Unida, 1973.

2369   *Hymns and Psalms: A Methodist and Ecumenical Hymn Book*. London: Methodist Publishing House, 1983.

2370   *Hymns From the Four Winds: A Collection of Asian American Hymns*. Supplemental Worship Resources 13. Nashville: Abingdon Press, 1983.

2371   *Methodist Pocket Hymn-Book*. Library of Methodist Classics. Nashville: United Methodist Publishing House, 1992. Facsimile of the 1793 printing of American Methodism's second official hymnal, first published in 1790.

2372   *Psalms for Praise and Worship*. Edited by John Holbert, S T Kimbrough, Jr., and Carlton R. Young. Nashville: Abingdon Press, 1992.

2373   *Psalms for Singing: Twenty-Six Psalms with Musical Settings for Congregation and Choir*. Translation of Psalms by Gary Chamberlain. Nashville: The Upper Room, 1984.

2374   *Songs of Zion*. Supplemental Worship Resources 12. Nashville: Abingdon Press, 1981. A songbook from the African American religious tradition.

2375   *The United Methodist Hymnal: Book of United Methodist Worship*. Nashville: United Methodist Publishing House, 1989.

2376   *The Upper Room Worshipbook: Music and Liturgies for Spiritual Formation*. Nashville: The Upper Room, 1985.

2377   *Voices: Native American Hymnal*. Nashville: Abingdon Press, 1992.

2378   Wesley, John. *A Collection of Hymns for the Use of the People Called Methodists*. Edited by Franz Hildebrandt and Oliver A. Beckerlegge. *The Works of John Wesley* (Bicentennial Edition), Vol. 7. Oxford: Clarendon Press, 1983; reprinted Nashville: Abingdon Press, 1990.

B. History and Commentary

2379 Berger, Teresa. *Theologie in Hymnen? Zum Verhältnis von Theologie und Doxologie am Beispiel der "Collection of Hymns for the Use of the People Called Methodists."* Altenberg: Telos Verlag, 1989.

2380 Cone, James H. *The Spirituals and the Blues: An Interpretation.* Philadelphia: Winston, 1972.

2381 Kimbrough, S T, Jr. *Lost in Wonder: Charles Wesley, the Meaning of his Hymns Today.* Nashville: The Upper Room, 1987.

2382 Lawson, John. *The Wesley Hymns as a Guide to Scriptural Teaching.* Grand Rapids, MI: Zondervan Publishing House, 1988.

2383 Lorenz, Ellen Jane. *Glory Hallelujah: The Story of the Camp Meeting Spiritual.* Nashville: Abingdon Press, 1980.

2384 Rattenbury, John E. *The Evangelical Doctrines of Charles Wesley's Hymns.* London: Epworth Press, 1941.

2385 ———. *The Eucharistic Hymns of John and Charles Wesley.* London: Epworth Press, 1948. Revised edition, Cleveland, OH: Order of St. Luke Publications, 1990.

2386 Rogal, Samuel J., comp. *Guide to the Hymns and Tunes of American Methodism.* New York: Greenwood Press, 1986. A reference guide to the 3,901 hymns and tunes included in six major Methodist hymnals, 1878 to 1964.

2387 Sanchez, Diana, ed. *The Hymns of The United Methodist Hymnal.* Nashville: Abingdon Press, 1989.

2388 Schilling, S. Paul. *The Faith We Sing.* Philadelphia: Westminster Press, 1983.

2389 Sizer, Sandra. *Gospel Hymns and Social Religion: The Rhetoric of Nineteenth-Century Revivalism.* Philadelphia: Temple University Press, 1978.

2390 Spencer, Jon Michael. *Protest and Praise: Sacred Music of Black Religion.* Minneapolis: Fortress Press, 1990.

2391 Warren, James I. *O For a Thousand Tongues to Sing: The History, Nature and Influence of Music in the Methodist Tradition.* Grand Rapids, MI: Francis Asbury Press of Zondervan Publishing House, 1988.

2392 Yoder, Don. *Pennsylvania Spirituals.* Lancaster. PA: Pennsylvania Folklore Society, 1961. A basic work on early EUB hymnody.

2393 Young, Carlton R. *Companion to the 1989 Hymnal.* Nashville: Abingdon Press, 1992. The basic work.

27. Missions

2394 Barclay, Wade C. *History of Methodist Missions.* 4 vols. New York: Board of Missions, The Methodist Church, 1949–1973.

2395 Behney, J. Bruce, and Paul H. Eller. *The History of the Evangelical United Brethren Church.* Nashville: Abingdon Press, 1979. Check index.

2396 Castro, Emilio. *Sent Free: Mission and Unity in the Perspective of the Kingdom.* Grand Rapids, MI: Wm. B. Eerdmans, 1985.

2397 *Grace upon Grace: The Mission Statement of The United Methodist Church.* Nashville: Graded Press, 1990. Mission statement adopted by the 1988 General Conference.

2398 Haines, J. Harry. *Committed Locally, Living Globally.* Nashville: Abingdon Press, 1982.

2399 Kehrburg, Norma. *Love in Action: UMCOR, 50 Years of Service.* Nashville: Abingdon Press, 1989.

2400 Maddox, Randy L. "Wesley as Theological Mentor: The Doctrine of Truth or Salvation through other Religions." *Wesleyan Theological Journal* 27/1 (1992). Forthcoming.

28. Native American Methodists

2401 Bowden, Henry W. *American Indians and Christian Missions: Studies in Cultural Conflict.* Chicago: University of Chicago Press, 1981.

2402 Copway, George. *Indian Life and Indian History.* New York: AMS Press, 1976. Reprint of the 1860 edition.

2403 Finley, James B. *Life Among the Indians; or, Personal Reminiscences and Historical Incidents Illustrative of Indian Life and Character.* Edited by D. W. Clark. New York: Ayer Co., 1976. Reprint of 1857 edition.

2404 Forbes, Bruce D. "'And Obey God, etc.': Methodism and American Indians." *Methodist History* 23/1 (October 1984): 3–24.

2405 ———. "Methodist Mission among the Dakotas: A Case Study of Difficulties." In *Rethinking Methodist History*, edited by Russell E. Richey and Kenneth E. Rowe, 48–58; see #2013.

2406 Grant, John Webster. *Moon of Wintertime: Missionaries and the Indians of Canada in Encounter since 1534*. Toronto: University of Toronto Press, 1984.

2407 Gray, C. Jarrett, Jr., comp. *The Racial and Ethnic Presence in American Methodism: A Bibliography*. Madison, NJ: General Commission on Archives and History, UMC, 1991.

2408 Hummelen, Remmelt, and Kathleen Hummelen. *Stories of Survival: Conversations with Native North Americans*. New York: Friendship Press, 1985.

2409 McLoughlin, William G. *Cherokees and Missionaries, 1789–1839*. New Haven: Yale University Press, 1984.

2410 Milner, Clyde A., and Floyd A. O'Neill, eds. *Churchmen and the Western Indians*. Norman, OK: University of Oklahoma Press, 1985. See especially article by Bruce Forbes on Methodist missions.

2411 Native American International Caucus. *The Sacred Circle of Life: A Native American Vision*. Norwalk, CA: Native American International Caucus, 1988.

2412 Noley, Homer, ed. *First White Frost: Native Americans and United Methodism*. Nashville: Abingdon Press, 1991. The basic work.

2413 Norwood, Frederick A. "The Invisible American: Methodism and the Indian." *Methodist History* 8/2 (January 1970): 3–24.

2414 "The United Methodist Church and America's Native People," 1980. In *The Book of Resolutions*, 1992.

29. Preaching

See also Part 3, Section 13: Ordained Ministry.

2415 Abbey, Merrill R. *The Epic of United Methodist Preaching: A Profile in American Social History*. Lanham, MD: University Press of America, 1984.

2416 Heitzenrater, Richard P. "Wesley as Preacher." In his *The Elusive Mr. Wesley*, 2:83–89; see #3050.

2417 ———. "Early Sermons of John and Charles Wesley." In his *Mirror and Memory: Reflections on Early Methodism*, 150–161; see #3051.

2418 Outler, Albert C. *John Wesley's Sermons: An Introduction*. Nashville: Abingdon Press, 1991. Originally published in *The Works of John Wesley* (Bicentennial Edition), 1:1–100.

2419 Spencer, Jon Michael. *Sacred Symphony: The Chanted Sermon of the Black Preacher*. New York: Greenwood Press, 1988.

2420 Wesley, John. "Address to the Clergy" (1756). In *The Works of John Wesley*, edited by Thomas Jackson, 10:480–500.

2421 ———. "Of Preaching Christ" (1751). In *The Works of John Wesley*, edited by Thomas Jackson, 11:486–492.

2422 ———. "Thoughts Concerning Gospel Ministers" (1784). In *The Works of John Wesley*, edited by Thomas Jackson, 7:455–456.

30. Publishing and Communications

2423 Cumbers, Frank H. *The Book Room: The Story of the Methodist Publishing House and Epworth Press*. London: Epworth Press, 1956.

2424 Ness, John H., Jr. *One Hundred Fifty Years: A History of Publishing in the Evangelical United Brethren Church*. Nashville: Abingdon Press, 1966.

2425 Pilkington, James P. *The Methodist Publishing House: A History*, Vol. 1. Nashville: Abingdon Press, 1968. The basic history to 1870. Continued by Walter N. Vernon, *The History of The United Methodist Publishing House*, Vol. 2. Nashville: Abingdon Press, 1988. The basic history from 1870 to 1968.

2426 Maynard, Edwin H. *Keeping Up with a Revolution: The Story of United Methodist Communications, 1940–1990*. Nashville: United Methodist Communications, 1990.

31. Social Thought

See also Part 3, Section 18: Theological Ethics.

2427 *The Book of Resolutions of the United Methodist Church, 1992*. Nashville: United Methodist Publishing House, 1992. Includes all valid resolutions since 1968 plus topical index.

2428 Brewer, Earl D. C., and Scott L. Thumma. *World Methodism and World Issues*. Atlanta: Center for Religious Research, Candler School of Theology, Emory University, 1990.

2429 Cameron, Richard M. *Methodism and Society in Historical Perspective*. Nashville: Abingdon Press, 1961.

2430 Gorrell, Donald K. *The Age of Social Responsibility: The Social Gospel in the Progressive Era, 1900–1920*. Macon, GA: Mercer University Press, 1988.

2431 ——. "The Social Creed and Methodism through Eighty Years." *Methodist History* 26/4 (July 1988): 213–228.

2432 Harkness, Georgia. *The Methodist Church in Social Thought and Action*. Nashville: Abingdon Press, 1972.

2433 *In Defence of Creation: The Nuclear Crisis and a Just Peace*. Nashville: Graded Press, 1986. The Bishops' Pastoral Letter, the foundation document, and guide for study and action.

2434 Letzig, Betty J. Expressions of Faith. Cincinnati: Service Center, General Board of Global Ministries, UMC, 1990. A study of the social welfare institutions of the National Division of GBGM.

2435 Muelder, Walter G. *Methodism and Society in the Twentieth Century*. Nashville: Abingdon Press, 1961.

2436 *On the History of the Methodist Federation for Social Service/Action*. Special issue of *Radical Religion* 5 (1980). Copies available from MFSA office.

2437 Seifert, Harvey. *What on Earth: Making Personal Decisions on Controversial Issues*. Nashville: Discipleship Resources for Church and Society, 1986.

2438 Stevens, Thelma. *Legacy for the Future: History of Christian Social Relations in the Woman's Division of Christian Service, 1940–1968*. Cincinnati: General Board of Global Ministries, UMC, 1978.

2439 Walsh, John D. "John Wesley and the Community of Goods." In *Protestant Evangelicalism: Britain, Ireland, Germany and America, 1750–1950: Essays in Honour of W. R. Ward*, edited by Keith Robbins, 25–50. Studies in Church History, Subsidia 7. Oxford: Blackwell, 1990.

2440 Ward, Alfred Dudley. *The Social Creed of The Methodist Church*. Revised edition. Nashville: Abingdon Press, 1965.

2441 Wesley, John. "The Danger of Riches" (1781). Sermon 87 in *The Works of John Wesley* (Bicentennial Edition), 3:227–246.

2442 ——. "The Nature, Design, and General Rules of the United Societies" (1743). See #2224.

2443 ——. "The Good Steward" (1768). Sermon 51 in *The Works of John Wesley* (Bicentennial Edition), 2:281–298.

2444 ———. "The Reformation of Manners" (1763). Sermon 52 in *The Works of John Wesley* (Bicentennial Edition), 2:300–323.

2445 ———. "Thoughts Upon the Present Scarcity of Provisions" (1773). In *The Works of John Wesley*, edited by Thomas Jackson, 11:53–59.

2446 ———. "The Use of Money" (1760). Sermon 50 in *The Works of John Wesley* (Bicentennial Edition), 2:263–282. Also in *John Wesley*, edited by Albert C. Outler, 238–250; see #3033.

2447 Will, Herman. *A Will for Peace: Peace Action in the United Methodist Church, A History.* Washington: General Board of Church and Society, UMC, 1984.

2448 Wilson, Robert W. *Biases and Blindspots: Methodism and Foreign Policy from World War II.* Wilmore, KY: Bristol Books, 1988.

[Sunday-schools: See Part 2, Section 13: Christian Education.]

32. Spirituality

See also Part 2, Section 15: Class Meetings, and Part 2, Section 34: Worship.

2449 Baker, Frank, ed. *The Heart of True Spirituality: John Wesley's Own Choice.* 2 vols. Grand Rapids, MI: Francis Asbury Press of Zondervan Publishing House, 1985–1986. Vol. 1: Selections from William Law; vol. 2: Selections from Thomas à Kempis, Pierre Poiret, Jean Duvergier de Hauranne, and Jacques Joseph Duguet.

2450 Bowyer, O. Richard, et al. *Prayer in the Black Tradition.* Nashville: Abingdon Press, 1986.

2451 Day, Albert E. *Discipline and Discovery: Workbook Edition.* Edited by Danny E. Morris. Nashville: The Upper Room, 1977.

2452 Harkness, Georgia. *Prayer and the Common Life.* Nashville: Abingdon-Cokesbury, 1948.

2453 Harper, Steve. *Devotional Life in the Wesleyan Tradition.* Nashville: The Upper Room, 1983.

2454 ———. *The Devotional Life of John Wesley, 1703–1738.* Doctoral dissertation, Duke University, 1981; Ann Arbor MI: University Microfilms International, 1981.

2455 Johnson, Susanne. *Christian Spiritual Formation in the Church and Classroom.* Nashville: Abingdon Press, 1989.

2456 Maas, Robin. *Crucified Love: The Practice of Christian Perfection.* Nashville: Abingdon Press, 1989.

2457 ——. "Wesleyan Spirituality: Accountable Discipleship." In *Spiritual Traditions for the Contemporary Church*, edited by Robin Maas and Gabriel O'Donnell, O.P., 303–331. Nashville: Abingdon Press, 1990.

2458 Outler, Albert C. "Spirit and Spirituality in John Wesley." *Quarterly Review* 8/2 (Summer 1988): 3–18.

2459 Palmer, Phoebe. *Phoebe Palmer: Selected Writings.* Edited by Thomas C. Oden. New York: Paulist Press, 1987.

2460 Saliers, Don E. *Worship and Spirituality.* Philadelphia: Westminster Press, 1985.

2461 ——. *The Soul in Paraphrase: Prayer and the Religious Affections.* Cleveland: Order of Saint Luke Publications, 1992.

2462 Schneider, A. Gregory. *The Way of the Cross Leads Home: Social Religion and Domestic Ideology in 19th Century Methodist Evangelicalism.* Bloomington, IN: Indiana University Press, 1992? Forthcoming.

2463 Selleck, J. Brian. "John Wesley and Spiritual Formation." *Doxology* 7 (1990): 6–16.

2464 Trickett, David. "Spiritual Vision and Discipline in the Early Wesleyan Movement." In *Christian Spirituality: Post-Reformation and Modern*, edited by Louis Dupré and Don E. Saliers, 354–371. New York: Crossroad, 1989.

2465 Wakefield, Gordon, ed. *The Fire of Love: The Spirituality of John Wesley.* London: Darton, Longman and Todd, 1976.

2466 ——. *Methodist Devotion: The Spiritual Life in the Methodist Tradition, 1791–1945.* London: Epworth Press, 1966.

2467 Wesley, John. *A Christian Library, Consisting of Extracts from and Abridgements of the Choicest Pieces of Practical Divinity which have been published in the English Tongue.* 30 vols. London: T. Blanshard, 1819–1827. First published in 50 volumes, 1749–1755. Wesley's prefaces only in *The Works of John Wesley*, edited by Thomas Jackson, 14:220–233.

2468 ——. "A Collection of Forms of Prayer for Every Day in the Week" (1733). In *The Works of John Wesley*, edited by Thomas Jackson, 11:203–259.

2469 ——. "A Collection of Prayers for Families" (1745). In *The Works of John Wesley*, edited by Thomas Jackson, 11:237–259.

2470 ——. *Devotions and Prayers of John Wesley.* Compiled and edited by Donald E. Demaray. Grand Rapids, MI: Baker Book House, 1977. Reprint of the 1957 edition.

2471 ———. "A Scheme of Self-Examination used by the First Methodists in Oxford." In *The Works of John Wesley*, edited by Thomas Jackson, 11:521–523. Also in *John and Charles Wesley*, edited by Frank Whaling, 85–87; see #2475.

2472 ———. *Wesley's Forms of Prayer*. Library of Methodist Classics. Nashville: United Methodist Publishing House, 1992. Facsimile reprint of the 1738 edition.

2473 Wesley, Susanna. *The Prayers of Susanna Wesley*. Edited and arranged by William L. Doughty. Grand Rapids, MI: Zondervan Publishing House, 1984. Reprint of the 1955 edition.

2474 *Wesleyan Spirituality in Contemporary Theological Education: A Consultation held October 17–19, 1987*. Nashville: Division of Ordained Ministry, General Board of Higher Education and Ministry, UMC, 1987.

2475 Whaling, Frank, ed. *John and Charles Wesley: Selected Prayers, Hymns, Journal Notes, Sermons, Letters, and Treatises*. Classics of Western Spirituality series. New York: Paulist Press. 1981.

2476 Wimberly, Edward P. "The Black Christian Experience and the Holy Spirit." *Quarterly Review* 8/2 (Summer 1988): 19–35.

A. Devotional Guides

2477 Consultation on Church Union. *Liberation and Unity*. Princeton, NJ: COCU, 1992–. Annual COCU Lenten study book.

2478 Job, Reuben P., and Norman Shawchuck. *A Guide to Prayer for All God's People*. Nashville: The Upper Room, 1991. Prayer companion to the Common Lectionary.

2479 ———. *A Guide to Prayer for Ministers and Other Servants*. Nashville: The Upper Room, 1983. Prayer companion to the Common Lectionary.

2480 *Prayer Calendar*. Edited by Sheila Bruton. Cincinnati: Service Center, General Board of Global Ministries, UMC, 1992. Daily guidance in prayer for the work and workers of the General Board of Global Ministries, published annually.

2481 *The Upper Room Disciplines*. Nashville: The Upper Room, 1992. Annual devotional manual.

2482   World Council of Churches. *Ecumenical Prayer Cycle: "With God's People."* Geneva: World Council of Churches, 1992–. Annual guide to prayer in 52 weekly sections. Each part of the world where Christian churches exist is lifted up with a simple map, a brief history of Christianity in that country or region, prayers from their churches' worship life, and a description of what issues Christians are struggling with there.

33. Women

For biographies of principal figures, see Part 2, Section 8.

2483   Born, Ethel W. *By My Spirit: The Story of Methodist Protestant Women in Mission, 1879–1939.* New York: Women's Division, General Board of Global Ministries, UMC, 1990.

2484   Brown, Earl Kent. *Women in Mr. Wesley's Methodism.* Lewiston, NY: Edwin Mellen Press, 1983.

2485   Campbell, Barbara. *In the Middle of Tomorrow.* New York: Women's Division, General Board of Global Ministries, UMC, 1975.

2486   Chilcote, Paul W. *John Wesley and the Women Preachers of Early Methodism.* ATLA Monograph Series No. 25. Metuchen, NJ: Scarecrow Press, 1991.

2487   Eltscher, Susan M., ed. *Women in the Wesleyan and United Methodist Traditions: A Bibliography.* Madison, NJ: General Commission on Archives and History, UMC, 1991.

2488   Fagan, Ann. *This is our Song: Employed Women in the United Methodist Tradition.* New York: Women's Division, General Board of Global Ministries, UMC, 1986. A history of the Wesleyan Service Guild.

2489   Gifford, Carolyn D., ed. *The American Deaconess Movement in the Early Twentieth Century.* New York: Garland Publishing, 1986. Includes Isabelle Horton's *The Burden of the City* (1904) and *The Early History of Deaconess Work and Training Schools for Women in American Methodism* (1911), with introductory essay by Gifford.

2490   ——, ed. *The Debate in the Methodist Episcopal Church Over Laity Rights for Women.* New York: Garland Publishing, 1986. Includes essays by James M. Buckley, George W. Hughey, Alpha J. Kynett, and Willis Palmer, with introductory essay by Gifford.

2491 ———, ed. *The Defense of Women's Right to Ordination in the Methodist Episcopal Church.* New York: Garland Publishing, 1986. Includes Frances Willard's *Woman in the Pulpit* (1889) and William F. Warren's "The Dual Human Unit: The Relationship of Men and Women According to Sociological Teachings of Holy Scripture" (1894), with introductory essay by Gifford.

2492 Gorrell, Donald K., ed. *Woman's Rightful Place: Women in United Methodist History.* Dayton, OH: United Theological Seminary, 1980. Reflects the EUB experience.

2493 Graham, E. Dorothy. *Chosen by God: The Female Itinerants of Early Primitive Methodism.* Birmingham: By the author, 1986. Doctoral dissertation, University of Birmingham, 1986.

2494 Hale, Harry, Jr., Morton King, and Doris M. Jones. *New Witnesses: United Methodist Clergywomen.* Nashville: Division of Ordained Ministry, General Board of Higher Education and Ministry, UMC, 1980.

2495 Hardesty, Nancy A. *Women Called to Witness: Evangelical Feminism in the 19th Century.* Nashville: Abingdon Press, 1984.

2496 Hoover, Theressa. *With Unveiled Face: Centennial Reflections on Women and Men in the Community of the Church.* New York: Women's Division, General Board of Global Ministries, UMC, 1983.

2497 Keller, Rosemary Skinner, et al., eds. *Methodist Women, A World Sisterhood: A History of the World Federation of Methodist Women.* [Cincinnati, OH]: World Federation of Methodist Women, 1986.

2498 ———, ed. *Spirituality and Social Responsibility: The Vocational Vision of Women in the Methodist Tradition.* Nashville: Abingdon Press, 1993. Forthcoming.

2499 ———, Hilah F. Thomas, and Louise L. Queen, eds. *Women in New Worlds: Historical Perspectives on the Wesleyan Tradition.* 2 vols. Nashville: Abingdon Press, 1981–82.

2500 Knotts, Alice G. *Bound by the Spirit, Found on the Journey: The Methodist Women's Campaign for Southern Civil Rights 1940– 1968.* Doctoral dissertation, Iliff School of Theology/University of Denver, 1989; Ann Arbor, MI: University Microfilms International, 1989.

2501 ———. "Race Relations in the 1920s: A Challenge to Southern Methodist Women." *Methodist History* 26 (July 1988): 199– 212.

2502 Kreutziger, Sarah S. *Going on to Perfection: The Contributions of the Wesleyan Doctrine of Entire Sanctification to the Value Base of American Professional Social Work through the Eyes of Nineteenth-Century Evangelical Women Reformers.* Doctoral dissertation, Tulane University, 1991; Ann Arbor, MI: University Microfilms International, 1991.

2503 McDowell, John Patrick. *The Social Gospel in the South: The Woman's Home Mission Movement in the Methodist Episcopal Church, South, 1886–1939.* Baton Rouge, LA: Louisiana State University Press, 1982.

2504 Myers, Sarah Joyce. *Southern Methodist Women Leaders and Church Missions, 1878–1910.* Doctoral dissertation, Emory University, 1990; Ann Arbor, MI: University Microfilms, 1990.

2505 Palmer, Phoebe. *The Promise of the Father; or, A Neglected Speciality of the Last Days.* Salem, OH: Schmul Publishers, 1981. Reprint of the 1859 edition; also reprinted New York: Garland Publishing, 1985. A massive defense of women's right to preach based on the promise of Joel 2:28.

2506 Reber, Audrie. *Women United in Mission: A History of the Woman's Society of World Service of the Evangelical United Brethren Church, 1946–1968.* Dayton OH: Otterbein Press, 1969. Available from Service Center, Board of Global Ministries, U M C, Cincinnati, OH.

2507 Rowe, Kenneth E. "Ordination of Women, Round One: Anna Oliver and the Methodist General Conference of 1880." *Methodist History* 12 (April 1974): 60–72.

2508 Schmidt, Jean Miller. *Grace Sufficient: A History of Women in American Methodism.* Nashville: Abingdon Press, 1993? Forthcoming.

2509 Stevens, Thelma. *Legacy for the Future: The History of Christian Social Relations in the Woman's Division of Christian Service, 1940–1968.* Cincinnati: Women's Division, General Board of Global Ministries, UMC, 1978.

2510 *They Went Out Not Knowing: An Encyclopedia of 100 Women in Mission.* New York: Women's Division, General Board of Global Ministries, UMC, 1986.

2511 *To a Higher Glory: The Growth and Development of Black Women Organized for Mission in The Methodist Church 1940–1968.* Cincinnati: Board of Global Ministries, UMC, 1978.

2512 *Words that Hurt and Words that Heal: Language about God and*

People. New edition. Nashville: Graded Press, 1991. Leader's guide plus full text of document prepared in 1988 by the United Methodist Task Force on Language Guidelines.

34. Worship

A. Service Books

2513 *The Book of Offices and Services after the Usage of The Order of Saint Luke*. Cleveland: Order of Saint Luke Publishing Office, 1988.

2514 *Ceremonies I and II*. 2 vols. New York: Women's Division, General Board of Global Ministries, UMC, 1983–1990.

2515 *The Daily Office, a Book of Hours for Daily Prayer*. 4 vols. Cleveland: Order of Saint Luke Publications, 1991–1994. Vol. 1: Advent, Christmas, Epiphany, Baptism of our Lord; Vol. 2: Lent through Easter Vigil; Vol. 3: Easter Vigil through the Great Fifty Days; Vol. 4: Trinity through Christ the King.

2516 *Handbook of the Christian Year*. Edited by Hoyt C. Hickman, et al. Nashville: Abingdon Press, 1992.

2517 *John Wesley's Prayer Book: The Sunday Service of the Methodists in North America*, with introduction, notes and commentary by James F. White. Cleveland: Order of Saint Luke Publications, 1992.

2518 *Lift Up Your Hearts: Eucharistic Prayers based on the Common Lectionary*. Edited by Michael J. O'Donnell. 3 vols. Cleveland: OSL Publications, 1989–1991. The Prayers of Great Thanksgiving patterned after those found in *The United Methodist Hymnal* 1989, with segments based on the texts of the Common Lectionary, Year A, B and C.

2519 *The Methodist Service Book*. London: Methodist Publishing House, 1975.

2520 *Ritual in a New Day: An Invitation*. Nashville: Abingdon Press, 1976.

2521 *The United Methodist Book of Worship*. Nashville: United Methodist Publishing House, 1992.

2522 *The United Methodist Hymnal: Book of United Methodist Worship*. Nashville: United Methodist Publishing House, 1989.

2523 *The Upper Room Worshipbook: Music and Liturgies for Spiritual Formation*. Nashville: The Upper Room, 1985.

B. History and Commentary

2524 Baker, Frank. *Methodism and the Love Feast*. London: Epworth Press, 1957.

2525 Bucke, Emory S., ed. *History of American Methodism*. See #2001, especially 1:312–316; 2:627–636; 3:174, 413–44, 473–474, 561–562, 610–612.

2526 Cooke, Richard J. *History of the Ritual of the Methodist Episcopal Church, with a Commentary on its Offices*. Cincinnati: Jennings & Pye; New York: Eaton & Mains, 1900.

2527 Costen, Melva W., and Darius L. Swann. "The Black Christian Worship Experience: A Consultation." *Journal of the Interdenominational Theological Center* 14 (Fall 1986/Spring 1987). Special issue.

2528 Davies, Horton. *Worship and Theology in England*, Vol. 3: *From Watts and Wesley to Maurice, 1690–1850*. Princeton: Princeton University Press, 1961. See especially 184–209.

2529 Elkins, Heather M. *Living on Borrowed Time: The Christian Calendar in 20th Century United Methodism*. Doctoral dissertation, Drew University, 1991; Ann Arbor MI: University Microfilms International, 1991.

2530 Harmon, Nolan B. "John Wesley's 'Sunday Service' and its American Revisions." *Wesley Historical Society Proceedings* 39 (June 1974): 137–144.

2531 ———. *The Rites and Ritual of Episcopal Methodism*. Nashville: Publishing House of the M.E.Church, South, 1926.

2532 Hickman, Hoyt C. *Companion to the Book of Services [1984]*. Nashville: Abingdon Press, 1989.

2533 ———. *United Methodist Worship*. Nashville: Abingdon Press, 1991.

2534 ———, ed. *The Worship Resources of the United Methodist Hymnal*. Nashville: Abingdon Press, 1989.

2535 Jennings, Theodore W., Jr. *The Liturgy of Liberation: The Confession and Forgiveness of Sins*. Nashville: Abingdon Press, 1988.

2536 McClain, William B. *Come Sunday: The Liturgy of Zion*. Nashville: Abingdon Press, 1990.

2537 Procter-Smith, Marjorie. *In Her Own Rite: Constructing Feminist Liturgical Tradition*. Nashville: Abingdon Press, 1990.

2538 Taylor, David L. "The Order of St. Luke and *The Versicle*: A Résumé, 1946–1961." *Doxology* 3 (1986): 48–56.

2539 Tucker, Karen B. Westerfield. *"Till Death Us Do Part": John Wesley's Services of Marriage and Burial and their Development in the Methodist Episcopal Church*. Doctoral dissertation, University of Notre Dame, 1992; Ann Arbor, MI: University Microfilms International, 1992.

2540 Wade, William N. *A History of Public Worship in the Methodist Episcopal Church and the Methodist Episcopal Church, South, from 1784 to 1905*. Doctoral dissertation, University of Notre Dame, 1981; Ann Arbor, MI: University Microfilms International, 1981.

2541 Watley, William D., ed. *The Word and Words: Beyond Gender in Theological and Liturgical Language*. Women's Task Force, Worship Commission of the Consultation on Church Union. Princeton: Consultation on Church Union, 1983.

2542 White, James F. *Protestant Worship: Traditions in Transition*. Louisville: Westminster/John Knox Press, 1989. See chapter 9, "Methodist Worship."

35. Youth

2543 Hutchinson, Paul. *The Story of the Epworth League*. Cincinnati: Methodist Book Concern, 1927.

2544 Smith, J. Warren. "Youth Ministry in American Methodism's Mission." *Methodist History* 19/4 (July 1981): 224–230.

2545 *The United Methodist Youth Fellowship Handbook*. Nashville: Discipleship Resources, 1989.

PART 3: DOCTRINE

1. Basic Doctrinal Statements
of The United Methodist Church

3001 *The Book of Discipline of The United Methodist Church*, 1988, Part II: "Doctrinal Standards and Our Theological Task," ¶¶66–69. Nashville: United Methodist Publishing House, 1988.

3002 *Doctrinal Standards and Our Theological Task.* Nashville: United Methodist Publishing House, 1988. Student book (reprint of Part II of 1988 *Discipline*) and leader's guide by Kenneth L. Carder.

2. Contemporary Discussions of Basic
Methodist Doctrines

3003 Carder, Kenneth L. *Sermons on United Methodist Beliefs.* Nashville: Abingdon Press, 1991

3004 *Foundations for Teaching and Learning in the United Methodist Church*, Nashville: Discipleship Resources, 1979.

3005 Heidinger, James V., ed. *Basic United Methodist Beliefs: An Evangelical View.* Wilmore, KY: Bristol Books, 1986.

3006 Jones, Ivor H., and Kenneth B. Wilson, eds. *Freedom and Grace.* London: Epworth Press, 1988.

3007 Kinghorn, Kenneth Cain. *The Gospel of Grace: The Way of Salvation in the Wesleyan Tradition.* Nashville: Abingdon Press, 1992.

3008 Langford, Thomas A., ed. *Doctrine and Theology in the United Methodist Church.* Nashville: Kingswood Books, 1990. Sets 1972 and 1988 doctrinal statements in historical context.

3009 ——. *God Made Known.* Nashville: Abingdon Press, 1992.

3010 Meeks, M. Douglas, ed. *What Should Methodists Teach? Wesleyan Tradition and Modern Diversity.* Nashville: Kingswood Books, 1990.

3011 Outler, Albert C. *Theology in the Wesleyan Spirit.* Nashville: Discipleship Resources, 1975.

3012 Runyon, Theodore H., ed. *Wesleyan Theology Today: A Bicentennial Theological Consultation.* Nashville: Kingswood Books, 1985.

3. John and Charles Wesley

A. Bibliography

3013 Baker, Frank. "Unfolding John Wesley: A Survey of Twenty Years Study in Wesley's Thought." *Quarterly Review* 1/1 (1980): 44–58.

3014 ——. *A Union Catalogue of the Publications of John and Charles Wesley*. Stone Mountain, GA: George Zimmermann, 1991. Reprint of the 1966 edition.

3015 Green, Richard. *The Works of John and Charles Wesley*. 2nd revised edition. New York: AMS Press, 1976. Reprint of the 1906 edition.

3016 Heitzenrater, Richard P. "The Present State of Wesley Studies." *Methodist History* 22 (1984): 221–231.

3017 Jarboe, Betty M. *John and Charles Wesley: A Bibliography*. Metuchen, NJ: Scarecrow Press, 1987.

B. Basic Texts

3018 *Charles Wesley's Earliest Sermons*. Edited by Thomas A. Albin and Oliver A. Beckerlegge. London: Wesley Historical Society, 1987. Six unpublished manuscript sermons.

3019 *Explanatory Notes upon the New Testament*. London: William Bowyer, 1755. Most recent reprint, Grand Rapids, MI: Baker Book House, 1987.

3020 *Explanatory Notes upon the Old Testament*. 3 vols. Bristol: William Pine, 1765. Facsimile reprint, Salem, OH: Schmul Publishers, 1975. A convenient one-volume reprint of both Old and New Testaments Notes is *Wesley's Notes on the Bible*, edited by G. Roger Schoenhals. Grand Rapids, MI: Francis Asbury Press of Zondervan Publishing House, 1987.

3021 *John Wesley's Sermons: An Anthology*. Edited by Albert C. Outler and Richard P. Heitzenrater. Nashville: Abingdon Press, 1991.

3022 *The Journal of the Rev. Charles Wesley*. Edited by Thomas Jackson. 2 vols. London: John Mason, 1949; reprinted Grand Rapids, MI: Baker Book House, 1980.

3023 *The Journal of the Rev. John Wesley*. Edited by Nehemiah Curnock. 8 vols. London: Epworth Press, 1909–1916. The standard annotated edition of the *Journal*; being replaced by the Bicentennial Edition of the *Journal and Diaries*, edited by W. Reginald Ward and Richard P. Heitzenrater; see #3028.

3024 *The Letters of the Rev. John Wesley.* Edited by John Telford. 8 vols. London: Epworth Press, 1931. The standard annotated edition of the *Letters*; being replaced by the much expanded and more accurate Bicentennial Edition of the *Letters*, edited by Frank Baker; see #3028.

3025 *A Plain Account of Christian Perfection.* London: Epworth Press; Philadelphia: Trinity Press International, 1990.

3026 *Poetical Works of John and Charles Wesley.* Edited by George Osborn. 13 vols. Salem, OH: Schmul Publishers, 1992? Forthcoming reprint of 1872 edition.

3027 *The Unpublished Poetical Writings of Charles Wesley.* Edited by S T Kimbrough, Jr., and Oliver A. Beckerlegge. 3 vols. Nashville: Kingswood Books, 1988–1992.

3028 *The Works of John Wesley.* Begun as "The Oxford Edition of the Works of John Wesley" (Oxford: Clarendon Press, 1975–1983); continued as "The Bicentennial Edition of the Works of John Wesley" (Nashville: Abingdon Press, 1984–). All volumes in print are now available from Abingdon Press. Referred to in these bibliographies as "(Bicentennial Edition)." Projected in 35 volumes; editors and dates given below for published volumes only:

Vol. 1–4: *Sermons.* Edited by Albert C. Outler (1984–1987).

Vol. 5–6: *Explanatory Notes Upon the New Testament.*

Vol. 7: *A Collection of Hymns for the Use of the People Called Methodists (1780).* Edited by Franz Hildebrandt and Oliver Beckerlegge (1983).

Vol. 8: *Worship and Prayer.*

Vol. 9: *The Methodist Societies, I: History, Nature and Design.* Edited by Rupert E. Davies (1989).

Vol. 10: *The Methodist Societies, II: The Conference.*

Vol. 11: *The Appeals to Men of Reason and Religion and certain Related Open Letters.* Edited by Gerald R. Cragg (1975).

Vol. 12: *Theological Treatises.*

Vol. 13: *The Defense of Christianity.*

Vol. 14–15: *Pastoral, Ethical, and Instructional Writings.*

Vol. 16: *Natural Philosophy and Medicine.*

Vol. 17: *Editorial Works.*

Vol. 18–24: *Journal and Diaries.* Edited by W. Reginald Ward and Richard P. Heitzenrater (1988–)

Vol. 25–31: *Letters.* Edited by Frank Baker (1980–).

Vol. 32: *Oxford Diaries.*

Vol. 33–34: *A Descriptive and Analytical Bibliography of the Publications of John and Charles Wesley.*

Vol. 35: *General Index and Miscellanea*

3029 *The Works of the Rev. John Wesley.* Edited by Thomas Jackson. 14 vols. London: Wesleyan Methodist Book Room, 1829–1831. Reprinted Grand Rapids, MI: Baker Book House, 1978. Has for years been the standard edition of Wesley's *Works*; now being replaced by the Bicentennial Edition; see #3028.

C. Selections

3030 Burtner, Robert W., and Robert E. Chiles, eds. *John Wesley's Theology: A Collection from his Works.* Nashville: Abingdon Press, 1982. Reprint of the 1954 edition entitled *A Compend of Wesley's Theology.*

3031 Jarboe, Betty M., comp. *Wesley Quotations: Excerpts from the Writings of John Wesley and other Family Members.* Metuchen, NJ: Scarecrow Press, 1990.

3032 Jay, Elisabeth, ed. *The Journal of John Wesley: A Selection.* New York: Oxford University Press, 1987.

3033 Outler, Albert C., ed. *John Wesley.* The Library of Protestant Thought. New York: Oxford University Press, 1964.

3034 Tyson, John R., comp. *Charles Wesley: A Reader.* New York: Oxford University Press, 1989.

3035 Watson, Philip S., ed. *The Message of the Wesleys: A Reader.* Grand Rapids, MI: Zondervan Publishing House, 1984. Reprint of 1964 edition.

3036 Whaling, Frank, ed. *John and Charles Wesley: Selected Prayers, Hymns, Journal Notes, Sermons, Letters and Treatises.* Classics of Western Spirituality. New York: Paulist Press, 1981.

D. Life and Thought

See also Part 2: History, Sections 2A & 2B.

3037 Baker, Frank. *Charles Wesley's Verse: An Introduction.* 2nd edition. London: Epworth Press, 1988.

3038 Campbell, Ted A. *John Wesley and Christian Antiquity: Religious Vision and Cultural Change*. Nashville: Kingswood Books, 1991.

3039 Cannon, William R. *The Theology of John Wesley, with Special Reference to the Doctrine of Justification*. Lanham, MD: University Press of America, 1984. Reprint of the 1946 edition.

3040 Cell, George C. *The Rediscovery of John Wesley*. Lanham, MD: University Press of America, 1984. Reprint of 1935 edition.

3041 Clapper, Gregory S. *John Wesley on Religious Affections: His Views on Experience and Emotion and their Role in the Christian Life and Theology*. Metuchen, NJ: Scarecrow Press, 1989.

3042 Collins, Kenneth J. *Wesley on Salvation: A Study in the Standard Sermons*. Grand Rapids, MI: Francis Asbury Press of Zondervan Publishing House, 1989.

3043 Clifford, Alan C. *Atonement and Justification. English Evangelical Theology, 1640–1790: An Evaluation*. Oxford: Clarendon Press, 1990.

3044 Coppedge, Allan. *John Wesley in Theological Debate*. Wilmore, KY: Wesley Heritage Press, 1988.

3045 Deschner, John. *Wesley's Christology: An Interpretation*. Dallas: Southern Methodist University Press, 1985. Reprint of 1960 edition with a new foreword by the author.

3046 Dowley, T. E. *Through Wesley's England*. Nashville: Abingdon Press, 1988. Colorful guidebook to Wesley's England.

3047 Gill, Frederick C. *Charles Wesley, the First Methodist*. London: Lutterworth Press, 1964.

3048 Green, V. H. H. *John Wesley*. Lanham, MD: University Press of America, 1987. Reprint of 1964 edition.

3049 Gunter, W. Stephen. *The Limits of "Love Divine": John Wesley's Response to Antinomianism and Enthusiasm*. Nashville: Kingswood Books, 1989.

3050 Heitzenrater, Richard P. *The Elusive Mr. Wesley*. 2 vols. Nashville: Abingdon Press, 1984.

3051 ——. *Mirror and Memory: Reflections on Early Methodism*. Nashville: Kingswood Books, 1989.

3052 ——. *Wesley and the People Called Methodists*. Nashville: Abingdon Press, 1993? Forthcoming. Indispensable.

3053 Jennings, Theodore W., Jr. *Good News to the Poor: John Wesley's Evangelical Economics*. Nashville: Abingdon Press, 1990.

3054 Jones, Scott. *John Wesley's Concept and Use of Scripture*. Doctoral dissertation, Southern Methodist University, 1992; Ann Arbor, MI: University Microfilms International, 1992.

3055 Kimbrough, S T, Jr., ed. *Charles Wesley: Poet and Theologian.* Nashville: Kingswood Books, 1992.

3056 Lindström, Harald. *Wesley and Sanctification: A Study in the Doctrine of Salvation.* Grand Rapids, MI: Francis Asbury Press of Zondervan Publishing House, 1982. Reprint of 1950 edition.

3057 Maddox, Randy L., ed. *Aldersgate Reconsidered.* Nashville: Kingswood Books, 1990.

3058 ———. *John Wesley: Practical Theologian of Responsible Grace.* Nashville: Kingswood Books, 1993? Forthcoming.

3059 Mickey, Paul A. *Essentials of Wesleyan Theology.* Grand Rapids, MI: The Francis Asbury Press of Zondervan Publishing House, 1980.

3060 Monk, Robert C. *John Wesley: His Puritan Heritage.* Nashville: Abingdon Press, 1966.

3061 Naglee, David I. *From Everlasting to Everlasting: John Wesley on Eternity and Time.* 2 vols. New York: Peter Lang, 1991–1992.

3062 Oden, Thomas C. *Wesley's Teaching.* 3 vols. Grand Rapids, MI: Zondervan Publishing House, 1992–1994. Forthcoming. Vol. 1: *Systematic Theology*; Vol. 2: *Pastoral Care*; Vol. 3: *Ethics and Society.*

3063 Outler, Albert C. *The Wesleyan Theological Heritage: Essays of Albert C. Outler.* Edited by Thomas C. Oden and Leicester R. Longden. Grand Rapids, MI: Francis Asbury Press of Zondervan Publishing House, 1991.

3064 ———. *Theology in the Wesleyan Spirit.* Nashville: Discipleship Resources, 1975.

3065 Pudney, John. *John Wesley and His World.* New York: Charles Scribner's Sons, 1978. Readable text, plus 125 excellent illustrations.

3066 Rack, Henry D. *Reasonable Enthusiast: John Wesley and the Rise of Methodism.* London: Epworth Press; Philadelphia: Trinity Press International, 1989.

3067 Rowe, Kenneth E., ed. *The Place of Wesley in the Christian Tradition.* Revised edition. Metuchen, NJ: Scarecrow Press, 1980. Reissue of 1976 edition with updated bibliography.

3068 Runyon, Theodore H. *The New Creation: John Wesley's Theology Today.* Nashville: Abingdon Press, 1993? Forthcoming.

3069   Sangster, William E. *The Path to Perfection: An Examination and Restatement of John Wesley's Doctrine of Christian Perfection.* London: Epworth Press, 1984. Reprint of 1943 edition.

3070   Schmidt, Martin. *John Wesley: A Theological Biography.* 2 vols. in 3. Nashville: Abingdon Press, 1962–1973.

3071   Stacey, John, ed. *John Wesley: Contemporary Perspectives.* London: Epworth Press, 1988.

3072   Starkey, Lycurgus M. *The Work of the Holy Spirit: A Study in Wesleyan Theology.* Nashville: Abingdon Press, 1962.

3073   Thorsen, Donald A. *The Wesleyan Quadrilateral: Scripture, Tradition, Reason & Experience as a Model of Evangelical Theology.* Grand Rapids, MI: Francis Asbury Press of Zondervan Publishing House, 1990.

3074   Tuttle, Robert G., Jr. *Mysticism in the Wesleyan Tradition.* Grand Rapids, MI: Francis Asbury Press of Zondervan Publishing House, 1989.

3075   Tyson, John R. *Charles Wesley on Sanctification: A Biographical and Theological Study.* Grand Rapids, MI: Francis Asbury Press of Zondervan Publishing House, 1986.

3076   Weyer, Michel. *Die Bedeutung von Wesleys Lehrpredigten für die Methodisten.* Stuttgart: Christliches Verlagshaus, 1987.

4. Otterbein

3077   Core, Arthur C., ed. *Philip William Otterbein: Pastor, Ecumenist.* Nashville: Abingdon Press, 1968. The principal theological texts plus commentary.

3078   O'Malley, J. Steven. *The Pilgrimage of Faith: The Legacy of the Otterbeins.* Metuchen, NJ: Scarecrow Press, 1973.

5. History of Biblical Interpretation

A. Major Methodist Bible Commmentaries

Arranged in alphabetical order. Commentaries on single books of the Bible have been excluded from this list.

3079   *1755:* Wesley, John. *Explanatory Notes upon the New Testament.* See #3019.

3080   *1765:* Wesley, John. *Explanatory Notes upon the Old Testament.* See #3020.

3081 *1801*: Coke, Thomas. *A Commentary on the Holy Bible*. 6 vols. London: G. Whitfield, 1801–1803. First and only American edition 1812.

3082 *1810*: Benson, Joseph. *The Holy Bible, with Notes, all the Marginal Readings, Parallel Texts, and Summaries of each Book and Chapter*. 5 vols. London: T. Blanshard, 1810–1815. Kept in print by American Methodist publishing houses until about 1880.

3083 *1810*: Clarke, Adam. *The Holy Bible, containing the Old and New Testaments, the Text Carefully Printed from the Most Current Copies of the present Authorized Version, including the Marginal Readings and Parallel Texts, with a Commentary and Critical Notes*. 8 vols. London: J. Butterworth & Son, 1810–1825. First American edition, 1811. Most recent reprint under the title *Clarke's Commentary*. 3 vols. Nashville: Abingdon Press, 1977.

3084 *1832*: Watson, Richard. *A Biblical and Theological Dictionary*. Revised by the American editors [Nathan Bangs, et al.]. New York: Published by B. Waugh and T. Mason for the Methodist Episcopal Church, 1832. Revised edition by T. O. Summers published by MEC, South, 1875. First published in London in 1831; last documented American Methodist printing in 1900.

3085 *1834*: ——. *An Exposition of the Gospels of St. Matthew and St. Mark, and of Some Other Detached Parts of Holy Scripture*. New York: Published by B. Waugh and T. Mason for the Methodist Episcopal Church, 1834. First published in London in 1833.

3086 *1839*: Longking, Joseph. *Questions on the Gospels: The Lessons in Historical and Chronological Order*. 4 vols. New York: T. Mason and G. Lane for the Sunday-school Union of the Methodist Episcopal Church, 1839. Companion volume: *Notes Illustrative and Explanatory on the Holy Gospels*. New York: G. Lane and P. P. Sandford for the Sunday-school Union of the Methodist Episcopal Church, 1841. Kept in print until at least 1865.

3087 *1853*: Strickland, William P. *Manual of Biblical Literature*. New York: Carlton & Phillips, 1853.

3088 *1860*: Whedon, Daniel D. *Commentary on the New Testament*. 5 vols. New York: Carlton & Porter; Cincinnati: Poe & Hitchcock, et al., 1860–80. Reprinted, Salem, OH: Schmul Publishers, 1977.

3089 *1869*: Summers, Thomas O. *Commentary on the Gospels.* 4 vols. Nashville: Southern Methodist Publishing House, 1869–1872. Commentary on Acts published 1882.

3090 *1873*: Whedon, Daniel D. *Commentary on the Old Testament.* 9 vols. New York: Nelson & Phillips, et al., 1873–1907. Reprinted, Salem, OH: Schmul Publishers, 1977.

3091 *1878*: Binney, Amos, and Daniel Steele. *The People's Commentary, including Brief Notes on the New Testament.* New York: Nelson & Phillips, 1878.

3092 *1879*: Vincent, John H., and Jesse L. Hurlbut. *The Lesson Commentary on the International Sunday-school Lessons for 1880–1888.* 8 vols. New York: Phillips & Hunt, etc., 1879–1887.

3093 *1888*: Drury, M. Richardson. *Handbook for Workers: A Manual of Bible Texts and Readings for use in Christian Work.* Dayton, Ohio: W. J. Shuey for the Church of the United Brethren in Christ, 1888. Available in German and English until 1897.

3094 *1895*: Meyer, Lucy Rider. *The Shorter Bible Chronologically Arranged, being the Holy Bible Abridged with its Writings Synchronized for Popular Reading.* New York: Hunt & Eaton, 1895. This Methodist "woman's Bible" was in print until 1912.

3095 *1905*: Hurlbut, Jesse L. *Christian Worker's Holy Bible.* Philadelphia: J. C. Winston Co., 1905.

3096 *1909*: Vincent, John H. *The Self-Interpreting Bible.* Saint Louis: Bible Education Society, 1909

3097 *1929*: *The Abingdon Bible Commentary.* Edited by Frederick C. Eiselen, Edwin Lewis, and David G. Downey. New York: Abingdon Press, 1929.

3098 *1951–1957*: *The Interpreter's Bible.* Edited by George A. Buttrick. 12 vols. New York: Abingdon-Cokesbury Press, 1951–1957.

3099 *1994*: *The New Interpreter's Bible.* Nashville: Abingdon Press, 1994–. Forthcoming.

B. Biblical Interpretation

3100 Clemons, James T. "John Wesley—Biblical Literalist?" *Religion in Life* 46 (1977): 332–342.

3101 Jones, Scott. *John Wesley's Concept and Use of Scripture.* Doctoral dissertation, Southern Methodist University, 1992; Ann Arbor, MI: University Microfilms International, 1992.

3102   Scroggs, Robin. "John Wesley as Biblical Scholar." *Journal of Bible and Religion* 28 (1960): 415–422.

3103   Stokes, Mack B. *The Bible in the Wesleyan Heritage*. Nashville: Abingdon Press, 1979.

6. History of Doctrine

For the Holiness movement, see Part 2, Section 24.

3104   Baker, Frank. "The Doctrines in the *Discipline*." In his *From Wesley to Asbury: Studies in Early American Methodism*, 162–182. Durham, NC: Duke University Press, 1976.

3105   Chiles, Robert E. *Theological Transition in American Methodism, 1790–1935*. Lanham, MD: University Press of America, 1984. Reprint of the 1965 edition.

3106   Cushman, Robert E. *John Wesley's Experimental Divinity: Studies in Methodist Doctrinal Standards*. Nashville: Kingswood Books, 1989.

3107   Deats, Paul, and Carol Robb, eds. *The Boston Personalist Tradition in Philosophy, Social Ethics, and Theology*. Macon, GA: Mercer University Press, 1986.

3108   Dunlap, E. Dale. *Methodist Theology in Great Britain in the 19th Century*. Doctoral dissertation, Yale University, 1956; Ann Arbor, MI: University Microfilms, 1968.

3109   Heitzenrater, Richard P. "At Full Liberty: Doctrinal Standards in Early American Methodism." In his *Mirror and Memory: Reflections on Early Methodism*, 189–204. Nashville: Kingswood Books, 1989.

3110   Holifield, E. Brooks. *The Gentlemen Theologians: American Theology in Southern Culture*. Durham, NC: Duke University Press, 1978. See especially 76–77, 140–143, 165–169, 186–202.

3111   Langford, Thomas A., ed. *Doctrine and Theology in the United Methodist Church*. Nashville: Kingswood Books, 1990. Sets 1972 and 1988 doctrinal statements in historical context.

3112   ———. *Practical Divinity: Theology in the Wesleyan Tradition*. Nashville: Abingdon Press, 1983. The basic survey.

3113   ———, comp. *Wesleyan Theology: A Sourcebook*. Durham, NC: Labyrinth Press, 1984.

3114 McCutcheon, William J. "American Methodist Thought and Theology, 1919–1960." In *History of American Methodism,* edited by Emory S. Bucke, 3:261–327; see #2001.

3115 Naumann, William H. *Theology and German-American Evangelicalism: the Role of Theology in the Church of the United Brethren in Christ and the Evangelical Association.* Doctoral dissertation, Yale University, 1966; Ann Arbor, MI: University Microfilms International, 1966.

3116 Norwood, Frederick A., ed. *The Methodist Discipline of 1798, including the annotations of Thomas Coke and Francis Asbury.* Rutland, VT: Academy Books, 1979.

3117 Oden, Thomas C. *Doctrinal Standards in the Wesleyan Tradition.* Grand Rapids, MI: Francis Asbury Press of Zondervan Publishing House, 1988.

3118 Outler, Albert C. "The Current Theological Scene: A View from the Beach at Ebb Tide." In World Methodist Conference (1966) *Proceedings,* 157–166. Nashville: World Methodist Council, 1966.

3119 ——. *Evangelism in the Wesleyan Spirit.* Nashville: Tidings, 1971. See especially Chapter 3, "A Third Great Awakening?"

3120 ——. *The Wesleyan Theological Heritage: Essays of Albert C. Outler.* Edited by Thomas C. Oden and Leicester R. Longden. Grand Rapids, MI: Francis Asbury Press of Zondervan Publishing House, 1991. See especially Part 2, "Spirit and Church in the Wesleyan Tradition," 145–250.

3121 Peters, John L. *Christian Perfection and American Methodism.* Grand Rapids, MI: Francis Asbury Press of Zondervan Publishing House, 1985. Reprint of the 1956 edition with a new foreword by Albert C. Outler.

3122 Runyon, Theodore H., ed. *Wesleyan Theology Today: A Bicentennial Theological Consultation.* Nashville: Kingswood Books, 1985.

3123 Scott, Leland. "The Concern for Systematic Theology, 1840–1870." In *History of American Methodism,* edited by Emory S. Bucke, 2:380–390; see #2001.

3124 ——. "The Message of Early American Methodism." In *History of American Methodism,* edited by Emory S. Bucke, 1:291–359; see #2001.

3125 ——. "Methodist Theology in America in the 19th Century." *Religion in Life* 25 (Winter 1955–1956): 87–98.

3126 ——. *Methodist Theology in America in the 19th Century.* Doctoral dissertation, Yale University, 1954.

3127 Shipley, David C. "The Development of Theology in American Methodism in the 19th Century." *London Quarterly & Holborn Review* 184 (1959): 249–264.

3128 ——. *Methodist Arminianism in the Theology of John Fletcher.* Doctoral dissertation, Yale University, 1942.

3129 Stoeffler, F. Ernest. "Pietism, the Wesleys and Methodist Beginnings in America." In his *Continental Pietism and Early American Christianity*, 184–221. Grand Rapids, MI: Wm. B. Eerdmans, 1976.

7. Representative Methodist Theologians Through 1992 (arranged chronologically)

3130 *1813*: Shinn, Asa. *An Essay on the Plan of Salvation.* Baltimore: Neal, Wilk & Cole, 1813.

3131 *1815*: Bangs, Nathan. *The Errors of Hopkinsianism Detected and Exposed.* New York: John C. Totten, 1815.

3132 *1826*: Watson, Richard. *Theological Institutes.* 2 vols. New York: N. Bangs and J. Emory for the Methodist Episcopal Church, 1826. First American edition from the first London edition 1823. "New edition" with index and "analysis" by John McClintock (New York: Lane and Scott for the Methodist Episcopal Church, 1850) is the most serviceable text, kept in print by the Methodist Book Concern until 1892.

3133 *1833*: Fletcher, John W. *Works.* 4 vols. New York: Waugh and Mason for the Methodist Episcopal Church, 1833. First American edition, 1833; reprinted Salem, OH: Schmul Publishers, 1984.

3134 *1837*: Fisk, Wilbur. *Calvinistic Controversy.* New York: Mason & Lane, 1837.

3135 *1840*: Binney, Amos. *Theological Compend, containing a System of Divinity.* New York: Mason & Lane, 1840. 1875 edition "improved" by Daniel Steele entitled *Binney's Theological Compend Improved.* New York: Phillips & Hunt; Cincinnati: Walden & Stowe, 1875.

3136 *1840*: Shinn, Asa. *The Benevolence and Rectitude of the Supreme Being.* Baltimore: Book Committee of the Methodist Protestant Church; Philadelphia: J. Kay & Brother, 1840.

3137   *1847*: Ralston, Thomas. *Elements of Divinity*. Nashville: A. H. Redford, 1847.

3138   *1850*: Palmer, Phoebe. *The Way of Holiness*. New York: Palmer & Hughes, 1850. Reprinted in *The Devotional Writings of Phoebe Palmer*, edited by Donald W. Dayton. New York: Garland Publishing, 1986.

3139   *1853*: Bledsoe, Albert T. *A Theodicy*. New York: Carlton & Phillips, 1853.

3140   *1853*: Jimeson, Allen A. *Notes on the Twenty-five Articles of Religion as Received and taught by Methodists in the United States, in which the Doctrines are carefully Considered and Supported by the Testimony of the Holy Scriptures*. Cincinnati: Applegate & Co., 1853.

3141   *1853*: Lowrey, Asbury. *Positive Theology, Being a Series of Dissertations on the Fundamental Doctrines of the Bible*. Cincinnati: Methodist Book Concern, 1853.

3142   *1856*: Arthur, William. *The Tongue of Fire; or, The True Power of Christianity*. London: Hamilton, Adams & Co.; New York: Harper & Brothers, 1856. One of the classic works of 19th-century Methodist theology. Reprinted regularly with an introduction by T. O. Summers by the Publishing House of the Methodist Episcopal Church, South, 1856–1926. Northern Methodists relied on Harper printings until 1896 when the Methodist Book Concern reissued it. The Methodist Book Concern kept the work in print until 1954. An abridged centenary edition was published in London by Epworth Press in 1956.

3143   *1856*: Lee, Luther. *Elements of Theology; or, An Exposition of the Divine Origin, Doctrine, Morals and Institutions of Christianity*. New York: Miller, Orton & Mulligan; Syracuse, NY: S. Lee, 1856.

3144   *1860*: Smith, George. *Elements of Divinity: A Series of Lectures on Biblical Science, Theology, Church History & Homiletics, Designed for Candidates for the Ministry, and other Students of the Bible*. Revised by T. O. Summers. Nashville: Southern Methodist Publishing House, 1860. In print until at least 1878.

3145   *1862*: Wakefield, Samuel. *A Complete System of Christian Theology; or, A Concise, Comprehensive and Systematic View of the Evidences, Doctrines, Morals and Institutions of Christianity*. New York: Carlton & Porter, 1862. Reprint, Salem, OH: Schmul Publishers, 1980.

3146 *1864*: Whedon, Daniel D. *The Freedom of the Will as Basis of Human Responsibility and a Divine Government.* New York: Carlton & Porter, 1864.

3147 *1875*: Pope, William B. *A Compendium of Christian Theology.* 2nd edition, revised and enlarged. 3 vols. New York: Phillips & Hunt, 1881. First London edition 1875–1876.

3148 *1877*: Raymond, Miner. *Systematic Theology.* 3 vols. New York: Nelson and Phillips, 1877–1879.

3149 *1877*: Winchell, Alexander. *Reconciliation of Science and Religion.* New York: Nelson & Phillips, 1877.

3150 *1880*: Curry, Daniel. *Fragments, Religious and Theological.* New York: Phillips & Hunt, 1880.

3151 *1882*: Merrill, Stephen M. *Aspects of Christian Experience.* Cincinnati: Walden & Stowe; New York: Phillips & Hunt, 1882. Revised edition: *Doctrinal Aspects of Christian Experience.* New York: Eaton & Mains, 1896.

3152 *1886*: Sheldon, Henry C. *System of Christian Doctrine.* Revised edition. New York: Harper & Brothers, 1886.

3153 *1887*: Banks, John A. *A Manual of Christian Doctrine.* London: T. Woolmer, 1887. Reissued by the Publishing House of the MEC, South 1897–1924.

3154 *1888*: Summers, Thomas O. *Systematic Theology.* Edited by John Tigert. 2 vols. Nashville: Publishing House of the Methodist Episcopal Church, South, 1888.

3155 *1891*: Foster, Randolph S. *Philosophy of Christian Experience.* New York: Hunt & Eaton, 1891.

3156 *1892*: Miley, John. *Systematic Theology.* 2 vols. New York: Hunt & Eaton, 1892–1894.

3157 *1893*: Rishell, Charles W. *The Higher Criticism; an Outline of Modern Biblical Study.* Cincinnati: Cranston & Stowe; New York: Eaton & Mains, 1893. Revised and enlarged edition, 1896.

3158 *1896*: Steele, Daniel. *A Defense of Christian Perfection.* New York: Hunt & Eaton, 1896; reprinted Salem, OH: Schmul Publishers, 1986.

3159 *1905*: Curtis, Olin A. *The Christian Faith.* New York: Eaton & Mains, 1905; reprinted Grand Rapids, MI: Kregel Publication, 1971.

3160 *1907*: Terry, Milton S. *Biblical Dogmatics.* New York: Eaton & Mains, 1907.

3161   *1908*: Bowne, Borden P. *Personalism*. Boston: Houghton, Mifflin & Co., 1908; reprinted New York: AMS Press, 1976.

3162   *1908*: Wheeler, Henry. *History and Exposition of the Twenty-five Articles of Religion of the Methodist Episcopal Church*. New York: Eaton & Mains; Cincinnati: Jennings & Graham, 1908.

3163   *1911*: Mains, George P. *Modern Thought and Traditional Faith*. New York: Eaton & Mains; Cincinnati: Jennings & Graham, 1911.

3164   *1913*: Gamertsfelder, Solomon J. *Systematic Theology*. Cleveland: C. Hauser, 1913. Revised edition, 1921.

3165   *1921*: Faulker, John A. *Modernism and the Christian Faith*. New York: Methodist Book Concern, 1921.

3166   *1923*: Mouzon, Edwin D. *Fundamentals of Methodism*. Nashville: Lamar & Barton, Agents, Publishing House, Methodist Episcopal Church, South, 1923.

3167   *1923*: Parker, Franklin N. *What We Believe: Studies in Christian Doctrine*. Nashville: Publishing House of the Methodist Episcopal Church, South, 1923.

3168   *1924*: Tillett, Wilbur F. *Personal Salvation*. Nashville: Cokesbury Press, 1924.

3169   *1926*: Rowe, Gilbert T. *The Meaning of Methodism*. Nashville: Cokesbury Press, 1926.

3170   *1927*: McConnell, Francis J. *The Christlike God: A Survey of the Divine Attributes from the Christian Point of View*. New York: Abingdon Press, 1927.

3171   *1930*: Knudson, Albert C. *The Doctrine of God*. New York: Abingdon Press, 1930.

3172   *1933*: ——. *The Doctrine of Redemption*. Nashville: Cokesbury Press, 1933.

3173   *1934*: Lewis, Edwin. *A Christian Manifesto*. Nashville: Cokesbury Press, 1934.

3174   *1936*: Rall, Harris F. *A Faith for Today*. Nashville: Cokesbury Press, 1936.

3175   *1940*: Brightman, Edgar S. *A Philosophy of Religion*. New York: Prentice-Hall, 1940. Reprinted, Westport, CT: Greenwood Press, 1972.

3176   *1947*: Harkness, Georgia. *Understanding the Christian Faith*. New York: Abingdon-Cokesbury, 1947; reprinted Nashville: Abingdon Press, 1981.

3177   *1950*: Ramsdell, Edward T. *The Christian Perspective*. Nashville: Abingdon-Cokesbury, 1950.

3178   *1951*: Nelson, John R. *The Realm of Redemption: Studies in the Doctrine of the Nature of the Church in Contemporary Protestant Theology*. Greenwich, CT: Seabury Press, 1951.

3179   *1952*: Turner, George A. *The More Excellent Way: The Scriptural Basis of the Wesleyan Message*. Winona Lake, IN: Light and Life Press, 1952. Revised edition: *The Vision Which Transforms: Is Christian Perfection Scriptural?* Kansas City, MO: Beacon Hill Press, 1964.

3180   *1953*: DeWolf, L. Harold. *A Theology of the Living Church*. New York: Harper & Brothers, 1953. Revised edition, New York: Harper & Brothers, 1960.

3181   *1953*: Rall, Harris F. *Religion as Salvation*. Nashville: Abingdon-Cokesbury, 1953.

3182   *1957*: Outler, Albert C. *The Christian Tradition and the Unity We Seek*. New York: Oxford University Press, 1957.

3183   *1959*: Michalson, Carl. *The Hinge of History: An Existentialist Approach to the Christian Faith*. New York: Charles Scribner's Sons, 1959.

3184   *1961*: Ogden, Schubert M. *Christ Without Myth: A Study Based on the Theology of Rudolph Bultman*. New York: Harper, 1961.

3185   *1965*: Rose, Delbert R. *A Theology of Christian Experience: Interpreting the Historical Wesleyan Message*. Minneapolis: Bethany Fellowship, 1965.

3186   *1965*: Cobb, John B., Jr. *A Christian Natural Theology: Based on the Thought of Alfred North Whitehead*. Philadelphia: Westminster Press, 1965.

3187   *1970*: Cone, James H. *A Black Theology of Liberation*. Philadelphia: J. B. Lippincott, 1970. 20th anniversary edition: Maryknoll, NY: Orbis Books, 1990; includes "After Twenty Years: Critical Reflections."

3188   *1971*: Jones, Major J. *Black Awareness: A Theology of Hope*. Nashville: Abingdon Press, 1971.

3189   *1972*: Wynkoop, Mildred B. *A Theology of Love: The Dynamics of Wesleyanism*. Kansas City, MO: Beacon Hill Press, 1972.

3190   *1975*: Míguez Bonino, José. *Doing Theology in a Revolutionary Situation*. Philadelphia: Fortress Press, 1975.

3191   *1975*: Outler, Albert C. *Theology in the Wesleyan Spirit*. Nashville: Tidings, 1975.

3192   *1976*: Cobb, John B., Jr. (with D. R. Griffin). *Process Theology: An Introductory Exposition.* Philadelphia: Westminster Press, 1976.

3193   *1979*: Oden, Thomas C. *Agenda for Theology: Recovering Christian Roots.* San Francisco: Harper, 1979. 10th anniversary revised edition: *After Modernity . . . What? Agenda for Theology.* Grand Rapids, MI: Zondervan Publishing House, 1990.

3194   *1979*: Ogden, Schubert M. *Faith and Freedom: Toward a Theology of Liberation.* Nashville: Abingdon Press, 1979. Revised and expanded edition, Nashville: Abingdon Press, 1989.

3195   *1980*: Wainwright, Geoffrey. *Doxology: The Praise of God in Worship, Doctrine and Life; A Systematic Theology.* New York: Oxford University Press, 1980.

3196   *1981*: Fowler, James W. *Stages of Faith: The Psychology of Human Development and the Quest for Meaning.* San Francisco: Harper & Row, 1981.

3197   *1981*: Cushman, Robert E. *Faith Seeking Understanding.* Durham: Duke University Press, 1981. Gathers together some of Cushman's most important essays, including "The Shape of Christian Faith—A Platform" (1956).

3198   *1986*: Ogden, Schubert M. *On Theology.* San Francisco: Harper & Row, 1986.

3199   *1987*: Oden, Thomas C. *Systematic Theology.* 3 vols. San Francisco: Harper & Row, 1987–1992. Vol. 1: *The Living God*; Vol. 2: *The Word of Life*; Vol. 3: *Life in the Spirit.*

3200   *1989*: Meeks, M. Douglas. *God the Economist: The Doctrine of God and Political Economy.* Minneapolis: Fortress Press, 1989.

3201   *1989*: Chopp, Rebecca S. *The Power to Speak: Feminism, Language, God.* New York: Crossroad, 1989.

3202   *1990*: González, Justo L. *Mañana: Christian Theology from a Hispanic Perspective.* Nashville: Abingdon Press, 1990.

3203   *1990*: Watson, David L. *God Does Not Foreclose: The Universal Promise of Salvation.* Nashville: Abingdon Press, 1990.

3204   *1991*: Cooper-Lewter, Nicholas, and Henry H. Mitchell. *Soul Theology: The Heart of American Black Culture.* Nashville: Abingdon Press, 1991.

3205   *1992*: González, Justo L. *Out of Every Tribe and Nation: Christian Theology at the Ethnic Roundtable.* Nashville: Abingdon Press, 1992.

3206 *1992*: Jennings, Theodore W., Jr. *Loyalty to God: The Apostles' Creed in Life and Liturgy.* Nashville: Abingdon Press, 1992.

3207 *1992*: Langford, Thomas A. *God Made Known.* Nashville: Abingdon Press, 1992.

3208 *1993*: Oden, Thomas C. *To Will and To Work: The Transforming Power of Grace.* Nashville: Abingdon Press, 1993. Forthcoming.

8. Oxford Institute of Methodist Theological Studies

3209 *First, 1959*: *Biblical Theology.* Selected essays published in *London Quarterly and Holborn Review* 184 (1959): 162–274.

3210 *Second, 1962*: *The Doctrine of the Church.* Edited by Dow Kirkpatrick. Nashville: Abingdon Press, 1964.

3211 *Third, 1965*: *The Finality of Christ.* Edited by Dow Kirkpatrick. Nashville: Abingdon Press, 1966.

3212 *Fourth, 1969*: *The Living God.* Edited by Dow Kirkpatrick. Nashville: Abingdon Press, 1971.

3213 *Fifth, 1973*: *The Holy Spirit.* Edited by Dow Kirkpatrick. Nashville: Tidings, 1974.

3214 *Sixth, 1977*: *Sanctification and Liberation: A Reexamination in the Light of the Wesleyan Tradition.* Edited by Theodore H. Runyon. Nashville: Abingdon Press, 1981.

3215 *Seventh, 1982*: *The Future of the Methodist Theological Traditions.* Edited by M. Douglas Meeks. Nashville: Abingdon Press, 1985.

3216 *Eighth, 1987*: *What Should Methodists Teach? Wesleyan Tradition and Modern Diversity.* Edited by M. Douglas Meeks. Nashville: Kingswood Books, 1990.

3217 *Ninth, 1992*: *Good News to the Poor in the Wesleyan Tradition.* Edited by M. Douglas Meeks. Nashville: Kingswood Books, 1994? Forthcoming.

9. Theological Education

3218 Cole, Charles E., ed. *Something More than Human: Leaders in American Methodist Higher Education.* Nashville: General Board of Higher Education and Ministry, UMC, 1986.

3219 McCulloh, Gerald O. *Ministerial Education in the American*

Methodist Movement. Nashville: General Board of Higher Education and Ministry, UMC, 1980.

3220 Miller, Glenn T. *Piety and Intellect: The Aims and Purpose of Ante-Bellum Theological Education*. Atlanta: Scholars Press, 1990.

3221 Patterson, L. Dale. *The Ministerial Mind of American Methodism: The Courses of Study for the Ministry of the Methodist Episcopal Church, the Methodist Episcopal Church, South and the Methodist Protestant Church, 1848-1920*. Doctoral dissertation, Drew University, 1984; Ann Arbor, MI: University Microfilms International, 1984.

3222 Wesley, John. "Address to the Clergy" (1756). In *The Works of John Wesley*, edited by Thomas Jackson, 10:480-500.

A. Seminary Histories

Asbury

3223 Shipps, Howard E. *A Short History of Asbury Theological Seminary*. Wilmore, KY: Asbury Theological Seminary, 1971.

Boston

3224 Cameron, Richard M. *Boston University School of Theology 1839-1968*. Boston: Boston University School of Theology, 1968. (*Nexus* 11/2-3, 1968.)

Drew

3225 Cunningham, John T. *University in the Forest: The Story of Drew University*. Florham Park, NJ: Afton Publishing Co., 1990.

3226 Richey, Russell E. "Drew Theological Seminary and American Methodism: Some Reflections." In *Scholarship, Sacraments and Service, Historical Studies in the Protestant Tradition: Essays in Honor of Bard Thompson*, edited by Daniel B. Clendenin and W. David Buschart, 89-104. Lewiston, NY: Edwin Mellen Press, 1990.

Duke

3227 Cushman, Robert E. "Fifty Years of Theology and Theological Education at Duke." *Duke Divinity School Review* 42/1 (Winter 1977): 3-22.

Emory (Candler School of Theology)

3228   Bowen, Boone M. *Candler School of Theology: Sixty Years of Service*. Atlanta: Candler School of Theology, Emory University, 1974.

Evangelical

3229   Eller, Paul H. *Evangelical Theological Seminary, 1873–1973, Shaping Ministry*. Naperville, IL: Evangelical Theological Seminary, 1973.

Gammon (Interdenominational Theological Center)

3230   Richardson, Harry V. *Walk Together, Children: The Story of the Birth and Growth of the Interdenominational Theological Center*. Atlanta: ITC Press, 1981.

Garrett

3231   Norwood, Frederick A. *Dawn to Midday at Garrett*. Evanston, IL: Garrett-Evangelical Theological Seminary, 1978.

Iliff

3232   Templin, J. Alton, ed. *An Intellectual History of the Iliff School of Theology, A Centennial Tribute 1892–1992*. Denver: Iliff School of Theology, 1992? Forthcoming.

Southern Methodist (Perkins School of Theology)

3233   Grimes, Lewis Howard. *A History of the Perkins School of Theology*. Edited by Roger Loyd. Dallas: Southern Methodist University Press, 1992.

Theologisches Seminar der Evangelisch-methodistischen Kirche, Reutlingen, Germany

3234   Klaiber, Walter, and Michel Weyer, eds. *Festschrift 125 Jahre Theologisches Seminar der Evangelisch-methodistischen Kirche, 1858–1983*. Reutlingen: Theologisches Seminar der Evangelisch-methodistischen Kirche, 1983.

United

3235   *United Theological Seminary Centennial Celebration: A Collection of Essays. United Theological Seminary Bulletin* 72/1 (January 1973). Dayton, OH: Union Theological Seminary, 1973.

Vanderbilt

3236 Conkin, Paul K. *Gone with the Ivy: A Biography of Vanderbilt University.* Knoxville, TN: University of Tennessee Press, 1985.

3237 Thompson, Bard. *Vanderbilt Divinity School: A History.* Nashville: Vanderbilt University, 1960.

Wesley

3238 Chandler, Douglas R. *Pilgrimage of Faith: A Centennial History of Wesley Theological Seminary, 1882–1982.* Edited by C. C. Goen. Cabin John, MD: Seven Locks Press, 1984.

10. Church

A. Basic Wesley Texts

Sermons:

3239 "Of the Church" (1785). Sermon 74 in *The Works of John Wesley* (Bicentennial Edition), 3:45–57.

3240 "On Schism" (1786). Sermon 75) in *The Works of John Wesley* (Bicentennial Edition), 3:58–69.

3241 "Catholic Spirit" (1750). Sermon 39 in *The Works of John Wesley* (Bicentennial Edition), 2:79–95.

3242 "On Laying the Foundation of the New Chapel, near the City Road, London" (1777). Sermon 112 in *The Works of John Wesley* (Bicentennial Edition), 3:557–592.

3243 "On Attending the Church Service" (1787). Sermon 104 in *The Works of John Wesley* (Bicentennial Edition), 3:464–478.

Tracts and Treatises:

3244 *The Methodist Societies: History, Nature and Design,* edited by Rupert E. Davies. *The Works of John Wesley* (Bicentennial Edition), Vol. 9 (1989).

Letters:

3245 "To Samuel Walker, September 24, 1755." In *The Works of John Wesley* (Bicentennial Edition), 26:592–596. Also in *John Wesley,* edited by Albert C. Outler, 73–76; see #3033.

3246 "To The Earl of Dartmouth, April 10, 1761." In *The Letters of John Wesley,* edited by John Telford, 4:146–152.

3247 "To Charles Wesley, August 18, 1785." In *The Letters of John Wesley*, edited by John Telford, 7:284–285.

3248 "To James Clark, July 3, 1756." In *The Letters of John Wesley*, edited by John Telford, 3:180–183.

B. Historical/Theological Studies

3249 Kirkpatrick, Dow, ed. *The Doctrine of the Church*. Nashville: Abingdon Press, 1964.

3250 Snyder, Howard A. *Models of the Kingdom*. Nashville: Abingdon Press, 1991.

3251 ——. *The Radical Wesley and Patterns for Church Renewal*. Downers Grove, IL: Inter-Varsity Press, 1980.

3252 ——. *Signs of the Spirit: How God Reshapes the Church*. Grand Rapids, MI: Academie Books, 1989.

11. Lay Ministry

3253 *The Book of Discipline*, 1992: "The Ministry of All Christians."

3254 Anderson, James D., and Ezra Earl Jones. *Ministry of the Laity*. San Francisco: Harper, 1983.

3255 Carter, William J. *Each One a Minister: A Bible Study and Guide for Action*. Nashville: Discipleship Resources, 1991.

3256 Chilcote, Paul W. *Wesley Speaks on Christian Vocation*. Nashville: Discipleship Resources, 1988.

3257 Edwards, Maldwyn. *Laymen and Methodist Beginnings Throughout the World*. Nashville: Methodist Evangelistic Materials, 1963.

3258 Harkness, Georgia. *The Church and its Laity*. Nashville: Abingdon Press, 1962.

3259 Norwood, Frederick A. *Church Membership in the Methodist Tradition*. Nashville: Abingdon Press, 1958.

12. Diaconal Ministry

3260 *The Book of Discipline*, 1992: "The Diaconal Ministry."

3261 Moore, Mary Elizabeth, Rosemary Skinner Keller, and Gerald F. Moede. *The Diaconate in the United Methodist Tradition*. Nashville: Division of Diaconal Ministries, General Board of Higher Education and Ministry, UMC, 1986.

13. Ordained Ministry

3262   *The Book of Discipline*, 1992: "The Ordained Ministry."

A. Basic Wesley Texts

Sermons:

3263   "On Obedience to Pastors" (1785). Sermon 97 in *The Works of John Wesley* (Bicentennial Edition), 3:373–383.

3264   "On the Death of John Fletcher" (1785). Sermon 114 in *The Works of John Wesley* (Bicentennial Edition), 3:610–629.

3265   "On Visiting the Sick" (1786). Sermon 98 in *The Works of John Wesley* (Bicentennial Edition), 3:387–397.

3266   "Prophets and Priests" ["The Ministerial Office"] (1789). Sermon 121 in *The Works of John Wesley* (Bicentennial Edition), 4:72–84.

Letters:

3267   "To James Hervey, March 20, 1739." In *The Works of John Wesley* (Bicentennial Edition), 24:609–610. Also in *John Wesley*, edited by Albert C. Outler, 70–73; see #3033.

3268   "To Samuel Walker, September 24, 1755." In *The Works of John Wesley* (Bicentennial Edition), 25:592–596. Also in *John Wesley*, edited by Albert C. Outler, 73–76; see #3033.

3269   "To Thomas Adam, October 31, 1755." In *The Works of John Wesley* (Bicentennial Edition), 25:609–611.

Essays:

3270   "Address to the Clergy" (1756). In *The Works of John Wesley*, ed. Thomas Jackson, 10:480–500.

3271   "Of Preaching Christ" (1751). In *The Works of John Wesley*, ed. Thomas Jackson edition, 11:486–492.

3272   "Thoughts Concerning Gospel Ministers" (1784). In *The Works of John Wesley*, ed. Thomas Jackson, 10:455–456.

B. Classic Texts

3273   Asbury, Francis. "A Valedictory Address to William McKendree, 1813" and "Address to the General Conference of 1816." In *The Journal and Letters of Francis Asbury*, edited by J. Manning Potts, 3:475–492; 3:531–542; see #2082.

3274   Clarke, Adam. *Preacher's Manual, including Clavis Biblica; or, A*

Compendium of Scriptural Knowledge, and his Letter to a Methodist Preacher on his Entrance into the Work of the Ministry; and also, Dr. Coke's Four Discourses on the Duties of a Minister of the Gospel. New York: Bangs and Mason for the Methodist Episcopal Church, 1821. A classic text kept in print by American Methodists, both north and south, until 1897.

3275 Coke, Thomas. *Four Discourses on the Duties of a Minister of the Gospel.* London: G. Whitfield; Philadelphia: John Dickins, 1798.

3276 Fletcher, John W. *Portrait of St. Paul; or, The True Model for Christians and Pastors.* London: T. Longman, 1790. First American Methodist printing, 1804; kept in print until 1896. Most recent reprint Salem, OH: Schmul Publishers, 1986.

C. Historical Studies

3277 Bowmer, John C. *Pastor and People: A Study of Church and Ministry in Wesleyan Methodism.* London: Epworth Press, 1975.

3278 Dunlap, E. Dale. "The United Methodist System of Itinerant Ministry." In *Rethinking Methodist History*, edited by Kenneth E. Rowe and Russell E. Richey, 18–28; see #2014.

3279 Grabner, John D. *A Commentary on the Rites of An Ordinal, The United Methodist Church [1980].* Doctoral dissertation, University of Notre Dame, 1985; Ann Arbor, MI: University Microfilms International, 1985. See Part I, "Episcopal Methodist Ordinal Revision 1784–1964," 1–158.

3280 Heitzenrater, Richard P. "A Critical Analysis of the Ministry Studies since 1944." *Occasional Papers issued by the United Methodist Board of Higher Education and Ministry* No. 76 (September 1, 1988).

3281 Holifield, E. Brooks. *A History of Pastoral Care in America: From Salvation to Self-Realization.* Nashville: Abingdon Press, 1983.

3282 McCulloh, Gerald O., ed. *The Ministry in the Methodist Heritage.* Nashville: Department of Ministerial Education, Board of Education, The Methodist Church, 1960.

3283 Mickle, Jeffrey P. "A Comparison of the Doctrines of Ministry of Francis Asbury and Philip William Otterbein." *Methodist History* 19 (July 1981): 187–205.

3284 Norwood, Frederick A. "The Shaping of Methodist Ministry."
Religion in Life 43 (Autumn 1974): 337–351.

3285 Outler, Albert C. "The Ordinal." In *Companion to the Book of
Worship (1966)*, 103–144. Nashville: Abingdon Press, 1970.

3286 ——. "Pastoral Care in the Wesleyan Spirit." In *The Wesleyan
Theological Heritage: Essays of Albert C. Outler*, edited by
Leicester R. Longden and Thomas C. Oden, 175–88.
Grand Rapids, MI: Francis Asbury Press of Zondervan
Publishing House, 1991.

3287 Steinmetz, David C. "Asbury's Doctrine of Ministry." In his
*Memory and Mission, Theological Reflections on the Christian
Past*, 82–95. Nashville: Abingdon Press, 1988.

D. Theological Studies

3288 Campbell, Dennis. *The Yoke of Obedience: The Meaning of Ordination in Methodism*. Nashville: Abingdon Press, 1988.

3289 Gerdes, Egon W. *Informed Ministry: Theological Reflections on
the Practice of Ministry in Methodism*. Zürich: Publishing
House of the United Methodist Church, 1976.

3290 Kohler, Robert F. *The Christian as Minister: An Inquiry into
Servant Ministry in the United Methodist Church*. 2nd edition.
Nashville: Division of Ordained Ministry, General Board of
Higher Education and Ministry, UMC, 1985.

3291 Messer, Donald E. *Contemporary Images of Christian Ministry*.
Nashville: Abingdon Press, 1989.

3292 ——, ed. *Send Me? The Itineracy in Crisis*. Nashville: Abingdon
Press, 1991. From their respective perspectives laypersons,
clergy spouses, clergy couples and bishops explore the
issues connected with itineracy, e.g. guaranteed appoint-
ments, freedom of the pulpit, open itineracy, etc.

3293 Oden, Thomas C. *Ministry Through Word and Sacrament*. New
York: Crossroad, 1988.

3294 ——. *Pastoral Theology: Essentials of Ministry*. San Francisco:
Harper & Row, 1983.

3295 UMC Commission to Study the Ministry, 1988–1992. "Report
to the 1992 General Conference." *Daily Christian Advocate*
(1992 advance edition).

3296 Yeager, Dick, ed. *A Manual for Pastor and Diaconal Ministers on
Developing and Evaluating an Effective Ministry*. Nashville:
Division of Ordained Ministry, General Board of Higher
Education and Ministry, UMC, 1986.

3297 ———, ed. *A Manual for Pastor (Staff) Parish Relations Committees on Developing and Evaluating an Effective Ministry.* Nashville: Division of Ordained Ministry, General Board of Higher Education and Ministry, UMC, 1986.

14. Episcopacy and Superintendency

3298 *The Book of Discipline*, 1992: "The Superintendency."

3299 Mathews, James K. *Set Apart to Serve: The Meaning and Role of Epsicopacy in the Wesleyan Tradition.* Nashville: Abingdon Press, 1985.

3300 *Messages of The Council of Bishops of The Methodist Church and The United Methodist Church during its Forty Years, 1939–1979.* Washington: Office of the Secretary of The Council of Bishops, 1979.

3301 Michell, Joseph. *There is an Election: Episcopal Elections in the Southeastern Jurisdiction of The United Methodist Church.* Troy, AL: Leader Press, 1980.

3302 Moede, Gerald F. *The Office of Bishop in Methodism: Its History and Development.* New York: Abingdon Press, 1964.

3303 Nelson, John R. "Methodism and the Papacy." In *A Pope for All Christians*, edited by Peter J. McCord, 148–175. New York: Paulist Press, 1975.

3304 *Position Papers and Documents, Council of Bishops, The Methodist Church 1965–1968, The United Methodist Church 1968–1984: A Bibliography.* Louisville, KY: Office of the Secretary of The Council of Bishops, UMC, 1986.

3305 Short, Roy H. *The Episcopal Leadership Role in United Methodism.* Nashville: Abingdon Press, 1985.

3306 ———. *History of The Council of Bishops of The United Methodist Church, 1939–1979.* Nashville: Abingdon Press, 1980.

3307 Yeager, Dick, ed. *Manual for District Superintendents on Developing and Supervising an Effective Ministry.* Nashville: General Board of Higher Education and Ministry, UMC, 1986.

15. Sacraments (General Studies)

3308 Borgen, Ole E. *John Wesley on the Sacraments.* Grand Rapids, MI: Francis Asbury Press of Zondervan Publishing House, 1986. Reprint of 1973 edition.

3309 Hickman, Hoyt C. *Workbook on Communion and Baptism*. Nashville: Discipleship Resources, 1990.

3310 Knight, Henry H., III. *The Presence of God in the Christian Life: A Contemporary Understanding of John Wesley's Means of Grace*. Metuchen, NJ: Scarecrow Press, 1992.

3311 Sanders, Paul S. *An Appraisal of John Wesley's Sacramentalism in the Evolution of Early American Methodism*. Doctoral dissertation, Union Theological Seminary, New York, 1954.

3312 ———. "The Sacraments in Early American Methodism." *Church History* 26 (1957): 355–371.

3313 Staples, Rob L. *Outward Sign and Inward Grace: The Place of Sacraments in Wesleyan Spirituality*. Kansas City: Beacon Hill Press, 1991.

3314 Wesley, John. "The Means of Grace" (1746). Sermon 16 in *The Works of John Wesley* (Bicentennial Edition), 1:376–397.

3315 White, James F. *Sacraments as God's Self-Giving*. Nashville: Abingdon Press, 1983.

16. Baptism/Confirmation

3316 Borgen, Ole E. "Baptism, Confirmation and Church Membership in the Methodist Church before the Union of 1968: A Historical and Theological Study." *Methodist History* 27 (1989): 89–109, 163–181.

3317 Cushman, Robert E. "Baptism and the Family of God." In *The Doctrine of the Church*, edited by Dow Kirkpatrick. Nashville: Abingdon Press, 1970.

3318 Felton, Gayle C. *This Gift of Water: The Theology and Practice of Baptism Among Methodists in America*. Nashville: Abingdon Press, 1992? Forthcoming.

3319 Good News. *We Believe: Confirmation and Membership Studies for United Methodists*. Wilmore, KY: Bristol Books, 1989. Junior High and Senior High/Adult editions plus teacher's guide.

3320 Hohenstein, Charles. *The Revisions of the Rites of Baptism in the Methodist Episcopal Church, 1784–1939*. Nashville: Kingswood Books, 1993? Forthcoming.

3321 Holland, Bernard. *Baptism in Early Methodism*. London: Epworth Press, 1970.

3322 Knight, Henry H., III. "The Significance of Baptism for the Christian Life: Wesley's Pattern of Christian Initiation." *Worship* 63/2 (March 1989): 133–142.

3323 Koehler, George E. *The United Methodist Member's Handbook.* Nashville: Discipleship Resources, 1987. Leader's guide, member's handbook, and filmstrip.

3324 "Lutheran-United Methodist Papers on Baptism." *Perkins Journal* 34 (Winter 1981): 1–56.

3325 "A Lutheran-United Methodist Statement on Baptism." *Quarterly Review* 1 (Fall 1980): 59–68. See also Lutheran and Methodist comment, 69–79. Statement and brief study guide available from Service Center, General Board of Global Ministries, UMC, Cincinnati, OH.

3326 Mutti, Fritz. *Faithful Members: The Doctrines and Duties of the Christian Faith.* Nashville: Graded Press, 1988. Resource for those entering the UMC by profession of faith or from other denominations. Student book and teacher guide.

3327 Naglee, David I. *From Font to Faith: John Wesley on Infant Baptism and the Nurture of Children.* New York: Peter Lang, 1987.

3328 Neinast, Helen R., and Sidney D. Fowler. *Journey into Faith: A Confirmation Resource for Junior Highs.* Nashville: Graded Press, 1984. Pastor's guide, student book and media kit.

3329 Stookey, Laurence H. *Baptism: Christ's Act in the Church.* Nashville: Abingdon Press, 1982. The basic work.

3330 UMC Baptism Study Committee. *By Water and the Spirit: A United Methodist Understanding of Baptism.* Nashville: Discipleship Resources, 1992. The text of the Committee's report to the 1992 General Conference, which may also be found in *Daily Christian Advocate* (1992 advance edition).

3331 Wesley, John. "The Marks of the New Birth" (1748) Sermon 18 in *The Works of John Wesley* (Bicentennial Edition), 1:415–430.

3332 ——. "The Great Privilege of those that are Born of God" (1748). Sermon 19 in *The Works of John Wesley* (Bicentennial Edition), 1:431–443.

3333 ——. "The New Birth" (1760). Sermon 45 in *The Works of John Wesley* (Bicentennial Edition), 2:186–201.

3334 ——. "Serious Thoughts Concerning Godfathers and Godmothers" (1752). In *The Works of John Wesley*, ed. Thomas Jackson, 10:506–509.

3335 ——. "Treatise on Baptism" (1758). In *The Works of John Wesley*, ed. Thomas Jackson, 10:188–201. Also in *John Wesley*, edited by Albert C. Outler, 318–332; see #3033.

3336   Willimon, William H. *Remember Who You Are: Baptism, a Model for Christian Life*. Nashville: The Upper Room, 1980.

3337   ——. *The Way: Confirmation for Discipleship in The United Methodist Church*. Nashville: Graded press, 1981. Pastor's manual and student book; available in Spanish and English.

3338   ——. *Your Child is Baptized*. Nashville: Discipleship Resources, 1988. Booklet designed for pastors to give to parents before or at the baptism of their children.

17. Lord's Supper

3339   Bowmer, John C. *The Sacrament of the Lord's Supper in Early Methodism*. London: Dacre, 1951. A classic.

3340   Elliott, Daryl M. "The Lord's Supper and the United Brethren in Christ." *Methodist History* 27/4 (July 1989): 211–229.

3341   Kriewald, Diedra, and Barbara Garcia. *Communion Book for Children*. Nashville: Discipleship Resources, 1984. Available in Spanish and English.

3342   Sanders, Paul S. "Wesley's Eucharistic Faith and Practice." *Anglican Theological Review* 148 (February 1966): 154–174. Reprinted in *Doxology* 5 (1988): 21–34.

3343   Stookey, Laurence H. *Eucharist: Christ's Feast with the Church*. Nashville: Abingdon Press, 1993? Forthcoming.

3344   Wainwright, Geoffrey. *Eucharist and Eschatology*. New York: Oxford University Press, 1982. Reprint of 1971 edition.

3345   Wesley, John. "The Duty of Constant Communion" (1732, reissued 1787). Sermon 101 in *The Works of John Wesley* (Bicentennial Edition), 3:427–439. Also in *John Wesley*, edited by Albert C. Outler, 332–344; see #3033.

3346   ——, and Charles Wesley. *Hymns on the Lord's Supper* (1745). 166 hymns plus a digest of Brevint's *Christian Sacrament and Sacrifice* (1673). For the latest critical edition, see John E. Rattenbury, *The Eucharistic Hymns of John and Charles Wesley* (Cleveland, OH: OSL Publications, 1990), a reprint of Rattenbury's 1948 edition rewritten in inclusive language. The *Hymns on the Lord's Supper*, an important appendix, remains untouched.

3347   Willimon, William H. *Sunday Dinner: The Lord's Supper and the Christian Life*. Nashville: The Upper Room, 1981.

18. Theological Ethics

See also Part 2, Section 31: Social Thought.

3348 Beach, Waldo, and H. Richard Niebuhr, eds. *Christian Ethics*. New York: Roland Press, 1955. See "John Wesley," 353–365.

3349 Birch, Bruce C., and Larry L. Rasmussen. *Bible and Ethics in the Christian Life*. Revised and expanded edition. Minneapolis: Augsburg, 1989.

3350 Gustafson, James. *Christ and the Moral Life*. Chicago: University of Chicago Press, 1968.

3351 Hauerwas, Stanley. *After Christendom: How the Church is to Behave if Freedom, Justice and a Christian Nation are Bad Ideas*. Nashville: Abingdon Press, 1991.

3352 ———. *Character and the Christian Life: A Study in Theological Ethics*. San Antonio, TX: Trinity University Press, 1975.

3353 ———. "Christianizing Perfection: Second Thoughts on Character and Sanctification." In *Wesleyan Theology Today*, edited by Theodore H. Runyon, 251–263; see #3015.

3354 ———, and William H. Willimon. *Resident Aliens: Life in the Christian Colony*. Nashville: Abingdon Press, 1989.

3355 Hulley, Leonard D. *To Be and To Do: Exploring Wesley's Thought on Ethical Behaviour*. Pretoria: University of South Africa, 1988.

3356 Hynson, Leon T. *To Reform the Nation: The Theological Foundations of Wesley's Ethics*. Grand Rapids, MI: Francis Asbury Press of Zondervan Publishing House, 1985.

3357 Jennings, Theodore W., Jr. *Good News to the Poor: John Wesley's Evangelical Economics*. Nashville: Abingdon Press, 1990.

3358 Jones, Major J. *Christian Ethics for Black Theology*. Nashville: Abingdon Press, 1974.

3359 McClendon, James W., Jr. *Ethics: Systematic Theology I*. Nashville: Abingdon Press, 1987.

3360 Marquardt, Manfred. *John Wesley's Social Ethics: Praxis and Principles*. Nashville: Abingdon Press, 1992.

3361 Ogletree, Thomas W. *The Use of the Bible in Christian Ethics: A Constructive Essay*. Philadelphia: Fortress Press, 1983.

3362 Rakestraw, Robert. *The Concept of Grace in the Ethics of John Wesley*. Doctoral dissertation, Drew University, 1985; Ann Arbor, MI: University Microfilms International, 1985.

3363   Seifert, Harvey. *What on Earth? Making Personal Decisions on Controversial Issues*. Nashville: Discipleship Resources for Church and Society, 1991.

3364   Wogaman, J. Philip. *Christian Moral Judgment*. Philadelphia: Westminster Press, 1989.

3365   ——. *Making Moral Decisions*. Nashville: Abingdon Press, 1990.

PART 4: POLITY

1. Basic Texts

4001 *The Book of Discipline of The United Methodist Church, 1992.* Nashville: United Methodist Publishing House, 1992. Available in English, Korean and Spanish.

4002 *The Decisions of the Judicial Council, 1968–1988.* Nashville: United Methodist Publishing House, 1989. For decisions 1989 and following, see appendix to the *General Minutes,* published annually.

4003 *Guidelines for Leadership in the Local Church, 1993–1996.* Nashville: Abingdon Press, 1992. 30 booklets developed by the Interagency Task Force on resources to provide guidance for the program and administration of the congregation.

2. Current Handbooks

4004 Tuell, Jack M. *The Organization of The United Methodist Church.* Revised 1992 edition. Nashville: Abingdon Press, 1993. Forthcoming.

3. History and Development

4005 Baker, Frank. "Polity." In *A History of The Methodist Church in Great Britain,* edited by Rupert E. Davies & Gordon Rupp, 1:211–256; see #2015.

4006 Behney, J. Bruce, and Paul H. Eller. *The History of the Evangelical United Brethren Church.* Nashville: Abingdon Press, 1979. Check index.

4007 Buckley, James M. *Constitutional and Parliamentary History of the Methodist Episcopal Church.* New York: Eaton & Mains, 1912.

4008 Davies, Rupert E. "Introduction" to *The Works of John Wesley* (Bicentennial Edition), Vol. 9: *The Methodist Societies, I: History, Nature and Design;* see #3031.

4009 Drinkhouse, Edward J. *History of Methodist Reform, Synoptical of general Methodism 1703–1789, with special and comprehensive reference to its most salient exhibition in the History of the*

Methodist Protestant Church. 2 vols. Baltimore: Board of Publication of the Methodist Protestant Church, 1899.

4010 Drury, Augustus W., ed. *The Disciplines of the United Brethren in Christ,* Dayton, OH: United Brethren Publishing House, 1895.

4011 Harmon, Nolan B. *The Organization of the Methodist Church.* 2nd revised edition. Nashville: United Methodist Publishing House, 1962. Originally published in 1948, this twice-revised book is the standard work on the history and development of Methodist polity.

4012 King, William M. "Denominational Modernization and Religious Identity: The Case of the Methodist Episcopal Church." *Methodist History* 20/2 (January 1982): 75–89.

4013 *Methodist General Rules and Disciplines.* Library of Methodist Classics. Nashville: United Methodist Publishing House, 1992. Facsimile reprints of Wesley's 1743 *General Rules* along with the first five books of discipline of the Methodist Episcopal Church, 1785–1789.

4014 Nickerson, Michael G. *Sermons, Systems and Strategies: the Geographic Strategies of the Methodist Episcopal Church in its Expansion into New York State, 1788–1810.* New Brunswick, NJ: Rutgers University Press, 1992? Forthcoming.

4015 Norwood, Frederick A., ed. *The Methodist Discipline of 1789, including the Annotations of Thomas Coke and Francis Asbury.* Rutland, VT: Academy Books, 1979. Facsimile reprint of the 1798 *Discipline* with notes and commentary by the church's first two bishops.

4016 Perry, Stephen. "The Revival of Stewardship and the Creation of the World Service Commission in the Methodist Episcopal Church 1912–1924." *Methodist History* 23/1 (July 1985): 223–239.

4017 Peterson, Peter A. *History of the Revisions of the Discipline of the Methodist Episcopal Church, South.* Nashville: Publishing House of the Methodist Episcopal Church, South, 1889.

4018 Primer, Ben. *Protestants and American Business Methods.* Ann Arbor, MI: UMI Research Press, 1979.

4019 Sherman, David. *History of the Revisions of the Discipline of the Methodist Episcopal Church.* New York: Hunt & Eaton, 1880.

4020 Tigert, John J. *Constitutional History of American Episcopal Methodism.* 6th edition, revised and enlarged. Nashville: Publishing House of the Methodist Episcopal Church, South, 1916.

4021 Wesley, John. "Minutes of the Conference 1744–1747." In *John Wesley*, edited by Albert C. Outler, 134–181; see #3033.

4022 ———. "The Nature, Design and General Rules of the United Societies" (1743). In *The Works of John Wesley* (Bicentennial Edition), 9:67–79. Cf. *The Book of Discipline*, 1988, Part II, ¶¶66–69.

4023 ———. "A Plain Account of the People called Methodists" (1749). In *The Works of John Wesley* (Bicentennial Edition), 9:253–280.

4024 Wilson, Robert L., and Steve Harper. *Faith and Form: A Unity of Theology and Polity in the United Methodist Tradition.* Grand Rapids, MI: Francis Asbury Press of Zondervan Publishing House, 1988.

PART 5: PERIODICALS

1. Bibliographies

5001 *A Checklist of British Methodist Periodicals*. Compiled by E. Alan Rose. London: World Methodist Historical Society Publications, 1981. 142 titles from 1778 to 1980.

5002 *Union List of United Methodist Serials 1773–1973*. Compiled by John and Lyda Batsel. Evanston: General Commission on Archives and History, UMC, with the United Methodist Librarians' Fellowship, and Garrett Theological Seminary, 1974.

2. Indexes

5003 *Methodist History Index, 1962–1982*. Compiled by Louise L. Queen. Madison, NJ: General Commission on Archives and History, UMC, 1982.

5004 *Methodist Reviews Index, 1818–1985*. Compiled by Elmer J. O'Brien. 2 vols. Nashville: General Board of Higher Education and Ministry, UMC, 1989. Vol. 1, Periodical Articles; Vol. 2, Book Reviews.

5005 *Religion Index One: Periodicals*. Chicago: American Theological Library Association, 1949–. Issues for 1949–1959 published as *Index to Religious Periodical Literature*.

5006 *The United Methodist Periodical Index*. Nashville: United Methodist Publishing House, 1961–1980. Issues for 1961–1965 published as *Methodist Periodical Index*. An important twenty year index to official United Methodist publications, including curriculum. No longer published.

5007 *Wesley Historical Society Proceedings: General Index to Vols 1–30 and Publications 1–4, 1897–1956*. Compiled by John A. Vickers. London: Wesley Historical Society, 1960.

3. The Current Basics

5008 *Christian Social Action*. Published monthly by the General Board of Church and Society.

5009 *Circuit Rider*. United Methodist clergy journal, published monthly by the United Methodist Publishing House.

5010 *The Interpreter.* Spanish version: *El Intérprete.* Korean version: *United Methodist Family.* Monthly program journals with news supplement published by United Methodist Communications.

5011 *Methodist History.* Published quarterly by the General Commission on Archives and History, UMC.

5012 *Quarterly Review.* A scholarly journal for reflection on ministry published by The United Methodist Publishing House and the General Board of Higher Education and Ministry, UMC.

5013 *United Methodist Newscope.* A national weekly newsletter for United Methodist leaders published by The United Methodist Publishing House.

5014 *United Methodist Reporter.* An independent national weekly newspaper published by United Methodist Communications Council, Dallas, Texas.

4. General Agency Periodicals

General Board of Church and Society:

5015 *Christian Social Action.*

5016 *Current Scene.*

5017 *DAC Bulletin: A Bulletin of Drug and Alcohol Concerns* (Dept. of Human Welfare).

5018 *Word from Washington* (Dept. of Field Service).

General Board of Discipleship:

5019 *Alive Now!* (The Upper Room).

5020 *El Aposento Alto* (The Upper Room).

5021 *Camp Memo* (Christian Education Section).

5022 *Church School Today* (Curriculum Resources Committee).

5023 *Covenant Discipleship Quarterly* (Section on Covenant Discipleship).

5024 *Curriculum Memo* (Curriculum Resources Committee).

5025 *Discipleship Trends* (Office of Research).

5026 *Discípulos Responsables.*

5027 *Ethnic Minority Local Church News Network* (Mission Priority Section).

5028 *Family Ministries Networker* (Section on Ministry of the Laity).

5029 *General Board of Discipleship Dateline* (Office of Communications & Interpretation).

5030 *Hallelujah!* (Section on Worship).

5031 *Horizons: Older Adult Ministry* (Section on Ministry of the Laity).

5032 *Information: Children's Ministries* (Section on Ministry of the Laity).

5033 *Jubilate, a Newsletter for United Methodist Musicians* (Section on Worship).

5034 *Lay Witness Newsletter* (Section on Evangelism).

5035 *Life Span* (Section on Ministry of the Laity).

5036 *Links* (Section on Ministry of the Laity).

5037 *The Living Prayer Newsletter* (The Upper Room).

5038 *Logos* (Section on Evangelism).

5039 *Men and Faith.*

5040 *MensNews* (United Methodist Men).

5041 *New Congregational Development* (Section on Evangelism).

5042 *Newsletter of Persons with Handicapping Conditions* (Jointly published by The Upper Room and the Division of Health and Welfare Ministries, General Board of Global Ministries, UMC).

5043 *Notes for Lay Leaders* (Section on Ministry of the Laity).

5044 *Peace Advocate* (Section on Ministry of the Laity).

5045 *People to People* (Curriculum Resources Committee).

5046 *Plain Talk About Lay Speaking* (Section on Ministry of the Laity).

5047 *Pockets* (The Upper Room).

5048 *Singles in Service* (Section on Ministry of the Laity).

5049 *Sunday School Extension Network* (Christian Education).

5050 *United Methodist News* (Korean).

5051 *United Methodist Stewardship Network Newsletter* (Section on Stewardship).

5052 *The Upper Room.*

5053 *Volunteer News* (The Upper Room).

5054 *Walk to Emmaus International Newsletter* (The Upper Room).

5055 *Weavings: A Journal of the Christian Spiritual Life* (The Upper Room).

5056 *Wings: A Newsletter on Disability, Aging and Christian Faith* (The Upper Room).

5057 *Worship Newsletter* (Section on Worship).

5058 *Young Adult Newsletter* (Section on Ministry of the Laity).

5059 *Youth Express* (NYMO).

5060 *Youth Ministry Resource Exchange* (Section on Ministry of the Laity).

5061 *Youth Servant Team Update* (Section on Ministry of the Laity).

General Board of Global Ministries:

5062 *Church and Community* (National Division).

5063 *Community Developers* (National Division).

5064 *Friends in Mission* (Mission Education Cultivation Program Dept.).

5065 *Health Ministry News* (Health & Welfare Ministries Program Dept.).

5066 *Inasmuch* (United Methodist Committee on Relief).

5067 *Mission News* (Mission Education Cultivation Program Dept).

5068 *Mission Papers*.

5069 *New World Outlook* (Mission Education Cultivation Program Dept.).

5070 *News and Views* (National Division).

5071 *Newsletter of Persons with Handicapping Conditions* (Jointly published by Health and Welfare Ministries and The Upper Room, General Board of Discipleship).

5072 *Response* (United Methodist Women).

5073 *740 Plan* (General Secretary).

5074 *Short-Term Volunteers in Mission* (Mission Personnel Resources Program Dept.).

5075 *Turning Points* (National Division).

5076 *U. M. Congress of the Deaf* (Health and Welfare Ministries Program Dept.).

5077 *UMCOR Update* (United Methodist Committee on Relief).

General Board of Higher Education and Ministry:

5078 *Access* (Division of Higher Education).

5079 *Across the Boards* (Division of Ordained Ministry).

5080 *Cite* (Association of United Methodist Theological Schools: Committee on Global Theological Education).

5081 *Coast to Coast* (Division of Higher Education).

5082 *Colleague* (Office of Interpretation).

5083 *Diaconal Dialogue* (Division of Diaconal Ministry).

5084 *Diaconal Report* (Division of Diaconal Ministry).

5085 *Ethnic Minority Clergy News* (Division of Ordained Ministry).

5086 *I. E.*, Newsletter of International Education (National Association of Schools and Colleges of the UMC).

5087 *Keepin' in Touch* (Division of Higher Education, Campus Ministry Section).

5088 *Impact* (Division of Chaplains and Related Ministries).

5089 *Lex Collegii* (Division of Higher Education).

5090 *New Perspectives* (Division of Higher Education).

5091 *New Witnesses* (Division of Ordained Ministry).

5092 *Occasional Papers* (Office of Interpretation).

5093 *On Board* (General Secretary's newsletter).

5094 *Orientation* (Campus Ministry Division).

5095 *Persons and Positions Available* (Division of Diaconal Ministry).

5096 *Presidential Papers* (Division of Higher Education).

5097 *Prism: A Quarterly for Retired United Methodist Clergy and Spouses* (jointly published with the General Board of Pensions).

5098 *Quarterly Review* (with U. M. Publishing House).

5099 *The Source* (Division of Ordained Ministry).

5100 *Update* (Division of Higher Education, Black College Fund).

5101 *Washington Newsletter* (Division of Higher Education).

5102 *Wellsprings, a Journal for United Methodist Clergywomen* (Division of Ordained Minsistry).

General Board of Pensions:

5103 *For Your Benefit.*

5104 *News & Views.*

5105 *Pension Updates.*

5106 *Prism: A Quarterly Journal for Retired United Methodist Clergy and Spouses* (jointly published with the Division of Ordained Ministry, General Board of Higher Education and Ministry, UMC).

General Commission on Archives and History:

5107 *Action Memo* (newsletter).

5108   *Methodist History* (scholarly journal). See index to Vols. 1–20, 1962–82.

General Commission on Religion and Race:
5109   *United Methodist Monitor.*

General Commission on the Status and Role of Women:
5110   *The Flyer.*

General Council on Finance and Administration:
5111   *Newsline* (local church insurance program newsletter).
5112   *Target* (insurance concerns).

General Council on Ministries:
5113   *Facts and Figures* (Office of Research).
5114   *Signs of the Times* (Office of Research).
5115   *Viewpoint* (Office of Research).

United Methodist Communications:
5116   *CW Update* (Circuit Writer Network).
5117   *Come/Share/Rejoice in Giving.*
5118   *El Intérprete.*
5119   *Interpreter.*
5120   *Keeping You Posted* (Dept. of Public Relations).
5121   *Methodists Make News.*
5122   *Network* (United Methodist Communicators).
5123   *News/News Service of the UMC.*
5124   *Pep-Talk Newsletter* (Division of Public Media).
5125   *TV/T Newsletter* (Television/Telecommunications Fund).
5126   *United Methodist Communicator* (Dept. of Public Relations).
5127   *United Methodist Family* (Korean-language program journal).

United Methodist Publishing House:
5128   *Church Library News* (Cokesbury).
5129   *Church Music Workshop.*
5130   *Church Secretary Newsletter* (Cokesbury).
5131   *Circuit Rider.*
5132   *Forecast* (Cokesbury). Quarterly catalog of resources for church, Sunday-school, and fellowship groups.

5133 *Leader in the Church School Today.*

5134 *The Magazine for Youth.*

5135 *Mature Years.*

5136 *Open Circuit.*

5137 *Quarter Notes for Leaders of Music with Children.*

5138 *Quarterly Review* (published jointly with General Board of Higher Education and Ministry).

5139 *Store Newsletter* (Cokesbury).

5140 *Teacher in the Church Today.*

5141 *United Methodist Newscope.*

5. Caucus Periodicals

Unofficial special interest/advocacy groups and affiliated groups. For addresses, see #1022, *The United Methodist Directory* (1992).

Affirmation, United Methodists For Lesbian, Gay and Bisexual Concerns:

5142 *Affirmation* (newsletter).

5143 *Mid-Atlantic Affirmation News.*

BMCR (Black Methodists For Church Renewal):

5144 *Now.*

Bush Meeting Dutch (an association for local history and genealogy of the former Evangelical United Brethren Church, its predecessors and sister churches):

5145 *Bush Meeting Dutch.*

Charismatics:

See #5178–5179 below.

Charles Wesley Society:

5146 *Charles Wesley Society Newsletter.*

Christian Educators Fellowship:

5147 *Professional Connection.*

Coalition of Black United Methodist Clergywomen:

5148 *Womanist Wisdom.*

Disciplined Order of Christ:

5149   *New Life News.*

**Fellowship of United Methodists in Worship,
Music and Other Arts:**

5150   *News Notes.*

Good News:

5151   *Catalyst* (newsletter for seminarians).
5152   *Good News.*

**Historical Society
of The United Methodist Church:**

5153   *Historian's Digest.*

International Church Computer Users Network:

5154   *Computers in the Church.*

**MARCHA (Methodists Associated Representing
the Cause of Hispanic Americans):**

5155   *Boletin de MARCHA.*

Methodist Federation for Social Action:

5156   *Social Questions Bulletin.*

Methodists United for Peace and Justice:

5157   *Peaceleaf.*

**Mexican American Program,
Perkins School of Theology:**

5158   *Apuntes.*

Mission Society for United Methodists:

5159   *Mission Advocate.*

**National Fellowship of Associate Members
and Local Pastors of the UMC:**

5160   *The Source* (newsletter).

National Filipino-American United Methodists:

5161   *Chronicle.*

National Japanese-American United Methodist Caucus:

5162   *Hono-o.*

National Women's Caucus of the UMC:

5163   *Yellow Ribbon.*

Native American International Caucus:

5164   *Echo of the Four Winds.*

Order of Saint Luke:

5165   *Doxology.*
5166   *The Font* (newsletter).
5167   *Sacramental Life.*

Professional Association for UM Church Secretaries:

5168   *PAUMCS Quarterly Newsletter.*

Reconciling Congregation Program:

5169   *Open Hands.*

Southern Asian National Caucus of United Methodists:

5170   *South Asian American News.*

Task Force of United Methodists
on Abortion and Sexuality:

5171   *Lifewatch.*

United Methodist Asian Caucus:

5172   *Asian American News.*

United Methodist Association
of Church Business Administrators:

5173   *UMACBA Newsletter.*

United Methodist Association
of Health and Welfare Ministries:

5174   *The Messenger.*

United Methodist Clergy Couples:

5175   *Clergy Couples Connect.*

United Methodist Fellowship of Healing:

5176 *Healing Frontiers.*

United Methodist Foundation for Evangelism:

5177 *Forward.*

United Methodist Renewal Services Fellowship
(Charismatic):

5178 *Manna.*
5179 *United Methodist Renewal Services Fellowship Notes.*

United Methodist Rural Fellowship:

5180 *United Methodist Rural Fellowship Bulletin.*

Wesleyan Theological Society:

5181 *Wesleyan Theological Journal.*

6. Theological Seminary Journals

Asbury Theological Seminary:

5182 *Asbury Theological Journal.*

Candler School of Theology, Emory University:

5183 *Ministry and Mission.*

Drew University Theological School:

5184 *Drew Gateway.*

Iliff School of Theology:

5185 *Iliff Review.*

Interdenominational Theological Center
(includes Gammon Theological Seminary):

5186 *Journal of the Interdenominational Theological Center.*

School of Theology at Claremont:

5187 *Occasional Papers.*

United Theological Seminary, Dayton:

5188 *Telescope-Messenger* (newsletter, The Center for the Evangelical
United Brethren Heritage).

5189   *Theological Journal.*

Wesley Theological Seminary:

5190   *Wesley Update.*

7. Larger Methodist Family in the US

5191   *A.M.E. Church Review.*

5192   *A.M.E. Zion Quarterly Review.*

5193   *Christian Index* (C.M.E. Church).

5194   *Herald of Holiness* (Church of the Nazarene).

5195   *Christian Recorder* (A.M.E. Church).

5196   *Light and Life* (Free Methodist Church).

5197   *Star of Zion* (A.M.E. Zion Church).

5198   *Wesleyan Advocate* (The Wesleyan Church).

8. World Methodist Family

For addresses, consult #1020, *Directory of World Methodist Publishing*, or contact: Periodicals Supervisor, Methodist Library, Drew University Theological School, Madison, NJ 07940; phone (201) 408-3590; fax (201) 408-3909.

5199   *Flame* (World Evangelism Committee of the World Methodist Council).

5200   *Historical Bulletin* (World Methodist Historical Society).

5201   *OxfordNotes* (Newsletter of the Oxford Institute of Methodist Theological Studies).

5202   *World Parish* (World Methodist Council).

Angola:

5203   *Ecos do Metodismo.*

Argentina:

5204   *El Estandarte Evangélico.*

Australia:

5205   *Frontier News* (news and information service).

5206   *Working Together* Nationally (agency annual).

5207   *World Mission Partners.*

5208 *Church Heritage* (Church Records and Historical Society, The Uniting Church in Australia, New South Wales Synod).

Austria:

5209 *Der Methodist.*

Benin/Togo:

5210 *Informations et Documentations.*

Bolivia:

5211 *Avance.*

5212 *Bolivian Echoes.*

5213 *Buenas Neuvas.*

5214 *Los Hechos.*

Brazil:

5215 *Expositor Christão.*

Canada:

5216 *United Church Observer* (principal monthly).

5217 *Mandate* (mission education magazine).

5218 *Bulletin of the Committee on Archives and History of The United Church of Canada.*

5219 *Canadian Methodist Historical Society Papers.*

5220 *Northwest Canada Echoes* (Northwest Canada Conference, The Evangelical Church).

Caribbean:

5221 *Advance* (Trinidad).

5222 *Jamaica Methodist Link.*

5223 *Leeward Islands Link.*

Chile:

5224 *El Cristiano.*

5225 *Vida y Mision.*

China:

5226 *China Talk* (Hong Kong China Liaison Office, World Division, General Board of Global Ministries, UMC).

5227 *Church News* (Church of Christ in China, Hong Kong).

Costa Rica:

5228   *Renuevos Metodistas.*

Czechoslovakia:

5229   *Slovo a Zivot.*

Denmark:

5230   *Kristelige Talsmand.*

Fiji:

5231   *Koniferedi.*

Finland:

5232   *Nya Budbararen.*
5233   *Rauhan Sanomia.*

France:

5234   *L'Évangeliste.*

Germany:

5235   *EMK Aktuell.*
5236   *Friedensglocke.*
5237   *Für Heute.*
5238   *Kinderzeitung.*
5239   *Mitarbeit.*
5240   *Mitteilungen der Studiengemeinschaft für Geschichte der Evangelisch-Methodistischen Kirche.*
5241   *Wort und Weg.*

Ghana:

5242   *Methodist Times.*

Great Britain:

5243   *Archives and History Newsletter.*
5244   *Cirplan* (Society of Cirplanologists).
5245   *Cliff Witness.*
5246   *Connexion* (Independent Methodists).
5247   *DSR News* (Methodist Church, Division of Social Responsibility).
5248   *Dunamis* (Charismatic fellowship).

5249 *Epworth Review*.

5250 *FK* (Fellowship of the Kingdom bulletin).

5251 *Facets* (Methodist Church, Overseas Division).

5252 *FUN: Follow-Up Notes to Window* (Methodist Church, Overseas Division).

5253 *Headline* (Evangelical caucus).

5254 *Local Preachers Magazine*.

5255 *Magnet* (Women's Network).

5256 *Methodist Church Music Society Bulletin*.

5257 *Methodist Librarians' Bulletin*.

5258 *Methodist Philatelic Society Bulletin*.

5259 *Methodist Recorder*, London (the principal weekly newspaper).

5260 *Methodist Sacramental Fellowship Bulletin*.

5261 *News and Views* (Home Missions Division).

5262 *NOW* (Methodist Church, Overseas Division).

5263 *Outline* (Methodist Church, Overseas Division).

5264 *Outside* (Methodist Church, Overseas Division).

5265 *Over to You* (Royal Navy, Army and Royal Air Force Board, Methodist Church).

5266 *Partners in Learning*.

5267 *React*.

5268 *Voice of Methodism*.

5269 *Wesley Historical Society Proceedings* (national and regional editions).

5270 *Wesleys's Chapel Magazine*.

5271 *Westminster Letter* (for clergy).

5272 *Window* (Methodist Church, Overseas Division).

5273 *Worship and Preaching*.

Hong Kong:

5274 *Church News* (Church of Christ in China).

5275 *Newsletter* (The Methodist Church, Hong Kong).

India:

5276 *Christian Education*.

5277 *Indian Witness* (Methodist Church in India, Lucknow).

5278 *Methodist Herald* (Methodist Church in India, Hyderbad).

5279 *North India Churchman* (Church of North India).

5280 *Methodist Pioneer* (Methodist Church in South India).

Indonesia:

5281 *Suara Methodist Indonesia.*

Ireland:

5282 *Methodist Newsletter* (Belfast).

Italy:

5283 *L'eco delle Valli Valdesi-La Luce.*

Korea:

5284 *Christian World.*

5285 *Theology and World/Sinhak Gwa Saige* (Methodist Theological Seminary, Seoul).

Liberia:

5286 *Circuit Rider* (Monrovia).

Malaysia:

5287 *Pelita Methodist.*

5288 *Southern Bell.*

Mexico:

5289 *Presencia.*

Mozambique:

5290 *Amigo do Pastor.*

New Zealand:

5291 *Crosslink.*

5292 *Focus.*

5293 *Wesley Historical Society, New Zealand Branch, Journal.*

5294 *Wesley Historical Society, New Zealand Branch, Newsletter.*

Nigeria:

5295 *Methodist News.*

Northern Ireland: see Ireland.

Norway:

5296 *Kristelige Talsmand.*

5297 *Teologisk Forum.*

Panama:

5298 *Enlace.*

Philippines:

5299 *Ang Ilaw* (The Light).
5300 *Methodist Reporter in the Philippines.*

Poland:

5301 *Pielgryzm Polski.*

Portugal:

5302 *Portugal Evangelico.*

Samoa:

5303 *Fetu Ao.*

Sierra Leone:

5304 *Methodist Bulletin.*
5305 *Methodist Diary.*
5306 *Sierra Leone Almanac.*
5307 *Sierra Leone Outlook.*
5308 *Sierra Leone Conference Newsletter.*

Singapore:

5309 *Methodist Message.*

South Africa:

5310 *Dimension.*
5311 *Dimension Supplement: Profile.*
5312 *Dimension Supplement: Cape Profile.*
5313 *Dimension Supplement: Natal Profile.*
5314 *Methodist Update.*

Sri Lanka:

5315 *Methodista Sakshiya* (Sinhala).
5316 *Sri Lanka Methodist Church Record.*
5317 *Thoduvanam* (Tamil).

Sweden:

5318 *Newsletter from Northern Europe.*
5319 *Svenska Sandebudet.*

Switzerland:

5320 *Kirche und Welt.*

Taiwan:

5321 *Wesley Periodical.*

Tonga:

5322 *Ko e Tohi Fanongonongo.*

United Kingdom: see Great Britain.

Uruguay:

5323 *Boletín Metodista.*

Zaire:

5324 *Dikendji.*

Zimbawe:

5325 *Nhume (The Messenger).*

PART 6: VIDEO RESOURCES

The following resources are available in the standard video formats. Many are available through annual conference audio-visual lending libraries and through EcuFilm, a United Methodist sponsored ecumenical film/video distribution service (address given in Part 8, below).

6001 *AIDS: A Healing Ministry.* Scenes from a national UM consultation on AIDS in San Francisco, November 1988. Produced for the Health and Welfare Ministries Program Department of the General Board of Global Ministries, 1989. 32 minutes. Distributed by EcuFilm.

6002 *Amazing Grace with Bill Moyers.* A moving history of this timeless hymn, features the Boys Choir of Harlem, Johnny Cash, Judy Collins, Jeremy Irons, Jessye Norman, Jean Ritchie and Marion Williams. Produced by PBS, 1990. Available from Hymn Society in the US and Canada Book Service, Fort Worth, TX.

6003 *Burning Bright.* Through a combination of live action photography and historic graphics this film presents major aspects of the history of The United Methodist Church and other churches of Methodist origin in the United States. Produced by United Methodist Communications and the General Commission on Archives and History, 1975. 32 minutes.

6004 *A Call to Serve.* Shows the variety of ways Diaconal ministers express their vocation and call. Produced by the Division of Diaconal Ministries, General Board of Higher Education and Ministry, 1988. 25 minutes.

6005 *Casting Out Fear: Reconciling Ministries with Gay/Lesbian United Methodists.* A provocative, warm video portraying the painful stories of lesbian and gay men in the church and the struggles of congregations to be welcoming. Produced by the Reconciling Congregation Program of Affirmation, United Methodists for Gay and Lesbian Concerns, 1988. 38 minutes.

6006 *A Charge to Keep: An Introduction to the United Methodist Church.* Narrated by William Willimon, this video introduces new and prospective church members to the UMC by focusing on four elements identified as UM strengths: fellowship, worship, Christian education and outreach. Produced by the United Methodist Publishing House, 1988. 30 minutes. Available from Cokesbury.

6007   *Claiming the Promise.* Three vignettes, which chronicle the story of three physically-challenged United Methodist pastors, dispels fears and doubts about the ability of persons with handicapping conditions to serve as church pastors. Produced by United Methodist Communications, 1991. 27 minutes.

6008   *Claiming the Story: A Journey in Christian History for United Methodists.* Privately produced for James E. Miller by Envisions (327 East Wayne St., Suite 250, Fort Wayne, IN, 46802), 1988. 35 minutes.

6009   *Class Leaders Teleconference.* Videotape of the live 90-minute teleconference on class leaders broadcast in May 1991. Produced by the Covenant Discipleship and Christian Formation Section of the General Board of Discipleship, 1991. 90 minutes.

6010   *The Community in Crisis: A Covenant Response.* Examines substance abuse confronting our communities; focuses on UM churches in the Washington, DC, area battling to reclaim young people and communities. Produced for the Bishops' Initiative on Drug Abuse, 1990.

6011   *Congregational Development: Four Videos.* A four-part series describing functions, accomplishments and goals of the various offices within the Congregational Development Unit of the National Program Division of the General Board of Global Ministries. Series titles: Congregational Development: A Challenge to Grow; Growth in Giving (Office of Finance & Field Service); Investing in Church Growth (United Methodist Development Fund); Building for Ministry & Mission (Office of Architecture). Produced by the National Program Division, GBGM. Each video is 15 minutes.

6012   *The Deaconess Story.* This well-researched video documentary explores the religious aspirations of the first generation of women who became Methodist Deaconesses (1890s). Using authentic photographs, music composed by participants in the movement, and personal recollections of women who remembered the early days, *The Deaconess Story* brilliantly captures the spirit, the substance, and the significance to women's history of this unique Protestant sisterhood. Privately produced in 1983 by Mary Agnes Dougherty and

History Media, 909 Carmel Ave., Albany, CA 94706. 12 minutes.

6013 *Discovering the Modern Methodists.* This two tape, 80-minute video narrated by David Lowes Watson contains a four part presentation on the early Methodist class meeting and modern covenant discipleship groups. Produced by the General Board of Discipleship, 1988. Part of Covenant Discipleship Congregation Kit. 80 minutes.

6014 *Frances Willard.* The story of her life and work. Produced by the Continuing Theological Education Department of Drew University Theological School, 1984. 30 minutes.

6015 *Francis Asbury.* The story of his life and ministry. Produced by the Continuing Theological Education Department of Drew University Theological School, 1983. 25 minutes.

6016 *From the Word Go.* This magazine format resource gives a variety of glimpses into the history and tradition of The United Methodist Church. It also captures contemporary images of United Methodist people. Produced by United Methodist Communications, 1984. 35 minutes.

6017 *A Gift of Song.* Produced for the celebration of the bicentennial of Methodism in America, this video features five choirs, chosen by their respective denominations, singing selections that reflect the evolution of American hymn singing. Produced for the Pan Methodist Bicentennial Committee by United Methodist Communications, 1984. 30 minutes.

6018 *The Good Mind.* Compares Native American and Christian religious expressions and theology. Produced by the United Methodist Publishing House, 1983. 30 minutes.

6019 *Images of Life/Visions of Hope.* Highlights four racial/ethnic local churches around the United States and their ministries to their communities. Produced by United Methodist Communications, 1986. 20 minutes.

6020 *In Defense of Creation.* Introduces the United Methodist Bishops' 1986 Pastoral Letter "In Defense of Creation: The Nuclear Crisis and the Pursuit of Peace." Produced by United Methodist Communications, 1986. 29 minutes.

6021 *John Wesley: The Proud Methodist.* Video biography of John Wesley privately produced for James Miller by Envisions, Fort Wayne, IN, 1988. 27 minutes.

6022 *A Lost History: 200 Years of Women in Methodism.* Interview format featuring Frances Willard, Anna Shaw, Harriet

Tubman, Mary Bethune, and others. Produced by NBC News and the National Council of Churches, 1985. 60 minutes.

6023 *Mission Magazine.* Up-to-date stories of the global mission work of the UMC. Produced by the General Board of Global Ministries, 1991. 30 minutes

6024 *No Longer Strangers.* Introduces the World Service Fund and The United Methodist Church as a global church. Produced by United Methodist Communications, 1987. 24 minutes.

6025 *One Faith, Many Visions,* Depicts United Methodist heritage and contemporary expressions of ministry. Produced by Wesley Theological Seminary, 1984. 30 minutes.

6026 *One World.* Video highlighting ecumenism through the World Council of Churches. Produced for the World Council of Churches, 1990.

6027 *The People Called Methodist.* Photographed in Australia, Singapore, Bolivia, Sierra Leone, Jerusalem and the United States, viewers see Methodists of many nationalities preaching, healing, and teaching in their own countries. Produced for the General Board of Global Ministries, 1991. 28 minutes. Available in Spanish and English.

6028 *Politeness and Enthusiasm, 1689–1791.* In the 18th century two forms of Christianity appeared: that of the elite—with an educated, "reasonable" God—and a more active form of Christianity, which discovered God to be gracious and experienceable. Essential background for understanding the rise of Methodism. Part of *The Christians* series, produced by McGraw-Hill Book Co., 1984. 38 minutes.

6029 *Portrait of Susanna.* Dramatic presentation of Susanna Wesley in an "Evening with" format. Produced by the Continuing Theological Education Department of Drew University Theological School, 1982. 35 minutes.

6030 *The Preacher: John Wesley.* Dramatic recreation of John Wesley preaching in the New Room, his famous chapel in Bristol, England. Produced by the BBC, 1981. 30 minutes.

6031 *Racism: The Church's Unfinished Agenda.* Highlights of National United Methodist Convocation on Racism, Sept. 1987. Produced for the General Commission on Religion and Race by EcuFilm, 1987.

6032 *Reflections on the Journey 1984–1988: Bishop Leontine T. C. Kelly.*

Produced by California/Nevada Conference Historical Society, Berkeley, CA, 1988. Autobiographical reflections of the UMC's first woman of color to be elected bishop.

6033   *Rejoicing in the Covenant.* Illustrates how annual conference benevolences share and extend World Service dollars. Produced for the General Council on Finance and Administration, 1991. 11 minutes.

6034   *The Revival of Hope.* Highlights what local churches in four Methodist denominations are doing to bring hope to their communities wracked by the drug crisis. Produced by the Pan-Methodist Coalition, 1991. Available from Cokesbury. 20 minutes.

6035   *The Richard Allen Story.* Produced for the bicentennial of the African Methodist Episcopal Church by Studio II Productions, Philadelphia, 1987. 35 minutes.

6036   *Service to the World.* The story of diaconal ministry in the United Methodist Church. Produced by the Division of Diaconal Ministry, General Board of Higher Education and Ministry,, 1986. 20 minutes.

6037   *Sharing the Heritage: The History of United Methodism in America.* Privately produced for James Miller by Envisions (327 East Wayne St., Suite 250, Fort Wayne, IN 46802) 1988. 32 minutes.

6038   *The Social Principles.* Bishop James S. Thomas, chairperson of the Social Principles Study Commission 1968–1972, discusses Biblical/theological foundations and answers frequently asked questions about the current Social Principles statement in the UMC Book of Discipline. Produced by the United Methodist Publishing House, 1990. 35 minutes.

6039   *The Structure of The United Methodist Church.* A graphic presentation of the UMC's organization for outreach, nurture, vocation, and advocacy, narrated by Nancy Grissom Self of the General Commission on the Status & Role of Women, 1989. 22 minutes.

6040   *Theressa Hoover: Through the Test of Time.* A moving video tribute to Theressa Hoover, who served for 22 years as deputy general secretary of the Woman's Division. Offers a vivid history of the organization and the women who created it. Produced for the Women's Division, General Board of Global Ministries, 1991.

6041   *This is Methodism.* Video of the story of Methodism in Great

Britain from John Wesley to the present day. Produced by the Methodist Publishing House, London, 1990.

6042 *Through Wesley's England.* Video tour follows the indefatigable Wesley to the key places he knew: Epworth, Oxford, London, Bristol, and other sites in the midlands and Yorkshire. Produced in England in 1988 by T.E.Dowley for the bicentennial of John Wesley's conversion. 30 minutes. Available from Cokesbury.

6043 *To Flourish and to Grow.* Video describing the Interdenominational Cooperation Fund and how this United Methodist general fund supports the World and National Council of Churches and the Consultation on Church Union. Produced by the General Commission on Christian Unity and Interreligious Concerns, 1990. 11 minutes.

6044 *To Live to God.* Introduction to the World Methodist Council and the World Methodist Museum, Lake Junaluska, NC. Produced by the World Methodist Council, 1985. 25 minutes.

6045 *UMCOR 50th Anniversary Video.* Shows how gifts to UMCOR through One Great Hour of Sharing and the Advance are bringing water to villages in Sumatra. Produced by United Methodist Communications for UMCOR, 1991.

6046 *Vital Congregations/Faithful Disciples.* Introduces the United Methodist Bishops' 1990 pastoral letter on church growth by highlighting varieties of "vital" congregations. Produced by the United Methodist Publishing House, 1990. Available from Cokesbury.

6047 *We are the Branches.* Explains how branch groups work and shows the impact that the experience has on young people. Produced cooperatively by the Office of Covenant Discipleship and Christian Formation, Section on Christian Education and Age-Level Ministries and the National Youth Ministry Organization, 1991. Available from Discipleship Resources.

6048 *Why I am a United Methodist.* In seven segments, enhancing the seven chapters in his book, *Why I am a United Methodist,* William Willimon leads viewers on a journey through the UMC. Willimon offers lively discussions of the history, theology, worship, and outreach of the denomination. Produced by the United Methodist Publishing House, 1990. 45 minutes. Available from Cokesbury.

6049 *Women Called to Ministry.* Introduces the Biblical and theological understandings of the ordination of women, sketches the history of clergywomen in the United Methodist tradition, and explores the current experience of local churches and clergywomen as they share in ministry. Produced by the Division of Ordained Ministry, General Board of Higher Education and Ministry, 1986. 30 minutes.

6050 *The World is Our Parish.* Introduces the ministry of the general agencies of The United Methodist Church. Produced by the General Council of Ministries, 1986. 25 minutes.

PART 7: BASIC LIBRARY FOR STUDENTS

1. The Basics

7001   *The Book of Discipline of The United Methodist Church,* 1992.

7002   *The Book of Resolutions of The United Methodist Church,* 1992.

7003   *The United Methodist Book of Worship,* 1992.

7004   *The United Methodist Hymnal,* 1989.

7005   Rowe, Kenneth E., ed. *United Methodist Studies: Basic Bibliographies.* 3rd edition, 1992.

2. History

7006   Heitzenrater, Richard P. *Wesley and the People Called Methodists.* Nashville: Abingdon Press, 1993? Forthcoming.

7007   González, Justo L., ed. *Each in Our Own Tongue: A History of Hispanic United Methodism.* Nashville: Abingdon Press, 1992.

7008   Guillermo, Artemio R., ed. *Churches Aflame: Asian-Americans and United Methodism.* Nashville: Abingdon Press, 1992.

7009   McEllhenney, John G., ed. *The Story of United Methodism in America.* Nashville: Abingdon Press, 1992.

7010   Noley, Homer, ed. *First White Frost: Native Americans and United Methodism.* Nashville: Abingdon Press, 1992.

7011   Norwood, Frederick A. *The Story of American Methodism.* Nashville: Abingdon Press, 1974.

7012   Schmidt, Jean Miller. *Grace Sufficient: A History of Women in American Methodism.* Nashville: Abingdon Press, 1993? Forthcoming

7013   Shockley, Grant S., ed. *Heritage and Hope: The African American Presence in United Methodism.* Nashville: Abingdon Press, 1992.

3. Doctrine

7014   Langford, Thomas A., ed. *Doctrine and Theology in the United Methodist Church.* Nashville: Kingswood Books, 1990.

7015 ——. *Practical Divinity: Theology in the Wesleyan Tradition.* Nashville: Abingdon Press, 1983.

7016 Meeks, M. Douglas, ed. *What Should Methodists Teach? Wesleyan Tradition and Modern Diversity.* Nashville: Kingswood Books, 1990.

7017 Outler, Albert C., ed. *John Wesley.* New York: Oxford University Press, 1964.

7018 Runyon, Theodore H. *The New Creation: John Wesley's Theology Today.* Nashville: Abingdon Press, 1993? Forthcoming.

7019 Wesley, John. *John Wesley's Sermons: An Anthology.* Edited by Albert C. Outler and Richard P. Heitzenrater. Nashville: Abingdon Press, 1991.

7020 Whaling, Frank, ed. *John and Charles Wesley: Selected Prayers, Hymns, Journal Notes, Sermons, Letters and Treatises.* Classics of Western Spirituality. New York: Paulist Press, 1981.

4. Polity

7021 *Guidelines for Leadership in the Local Church 1993–1996.* 30 booklets. Nashville: United Methodist Publishing House, 1992. Forthcoming.

7022 Tuell, Jack M. *The Organization of The United Methodist Church.* Revised 1993 edition. Nashville: Abingdon Press, 1993. Forthcoming.

5. Periodicals

7023 *Christian Social Action* (social thought journal).

7024 *Circuit Rider* (clergy journal).

7025 *The Interpreter* (Spanish version: *El Intérprete*; Korean version: *United Methodist Family*; program journals).

7026 *Methodist History* (historical journal).

7027 *Quarterly Review* (theological journal).

7028 *United Methodist Newscope* (weekly newsletter).

7029 *United Methodist Reporter* (weekly newspaper).

PART 8: ADDRESSES AND TELEPHONE NUMBERS OF PRINCIPAL SUPPLIERS

For Methodist publishers outside the US and UK see #1020, *Directory of World Methodist Publishing*. For out-of-print Methodist books, see the book dealers listed below.

8001 Abingdon Press/United Methodist Publishing House
      Customer Service Department
      201 Eighth Avenue, South
      P.O. Box 801
      Nashville, TN 37202-0801
      Phone: (800) 251-3320

8002 Cokesbury Mail Order Center
      201 Eighth Avenue, South
      Nashville, TN 37203
      Phone: (800) 672-1789

8003 Discipleship Resources
      Customer Services
      1908 Grand Ave.
      P.O.Box 189
      Nashville, TN 37202-0189
      Phone: (615) 340-7284

8004 EcuFilm
      810 12th Ave., South
      Nashville, TN 37203-4744
      Phone: (800) 251-4091

8005 Epworth Press (England)
      c/o Trinity Press International
      3725 Chestnut Street
      Philadelphia, PA 19104
      Phone: (800) 421-8874

General Board of Church and Society, see Discipleship Resources

8006 General Board of Global Ministries
      Service Center
      7820 Reading Road
      Cincinnati, OH 45222-1800
      Phone: (513) 761-2100

Kingswood Books, see Abingdon Press

8007   Methodist Publishing House (England)
       20 Ivatt Way
       Peterborough
       ENGLAND PE3 7PG
       Phone (from US): 011-44-733-332202

United Methodist Publishing House, see Abingdon Press

8008   The Upper Room
       Customer Services
       P.O. Box 189
       Nashville, TN 37202-0189
       Phone: (615) 340-7290

Out-of-Print Sources

8009   Gage Postal Books
       P.O. Box 105
       Westcliff-on-Sea
       Essex SS0 8EQ
       ENGLAND
       Phone (from US): 011-44-702-715133

8010   Charles A. Green
       P.O. Box 6095
       Philadelphia, PA 19114-0695
       Phone: (215) 824-1425

8011   Noah's Ark Book Attic
       Stony Point, Route 2
       Greenwood, SC 29646
       Phone: (803) 374-3013

8012   Phyllis Tholin Books (women's studies only)
       824 Ridge Terrace
       Evanston, IL 60201
       Phone: (312) 475-1174

8013   George A. Zimmermann, Jr.
       4219 Colony East Drive
       Stone Mountain, GA 30083
       Phone: (404) 288-8469

AUTHOR/EDITOR INDEX

This index lists the authors and/or editors of the major works cited in these bibliographies by item number. It is intended primarily to serve as a guide for locating the works of a particular individual. For this reason, works produced by the boards, agencies, or organizations of the Church are not included in this index, nor are works by John or Charles Wesley. When a particular work is cited more than once, each citation carries a different item number.

Pudney, John, 3065
Queen, Louise L., 2498, 5003
Raboteau, Albert J., 2169
Rack, Henry D., 1014, 3066
Rakestraw, Robert, 3362
Rall, Harris F., 3174, 3181
Ralston, Thomas, 3137
Ramsdell, Edward T., 3177
Rasmussen, Larry L., 3349
Rattenbury, John E., 2384, 2385
Raymond, Miner, 3148
Reames, Cheryl W., 2049
Reber, Audrie, 2506
Reid, Alexander J., 2051
Richardson, Harry V., 2170, 3230
Richey, Russell E., 2011, 2014, 2229, 3226
Rishell, Charles W., 3157
Robb, Carol, 3107
Rogal, Samuel J., 2386
Rogers, Harold, 2093
Rose, Delbert R., 3185
Rose, E. Alan, 5001
Rowe, Kenneth E., 1015, 1016, 1017, 2014, 2507, 3067
Rowe, Gilbert T., 3169
Rudolph, L. C., 2083
Runyon, Daniel V., 2198
Runyon, Theodore H., 3012, 3068, 3122, 3214, 7018
Rupp, Gordon, 2017, 2028
Russalesi, Steven D., 2280
Ryan, Roy H., 2208
Saliers, Don E., 2460, 2461
Sanchez, Diana, 2387
Sánchez, Gildo, 2073
Sanders, Paul S., 3311, 3312, 3342
Sanderson, Joseph E., 2005
Sangster, William E., 3069
Sano, Roy I., 2290
Schilling, S. Paul, 2388
Schisler, John Q., 2209
Schmidt, Jean Miller, 2508, 7012
Schmidt, Martin, 3070
Schneider, A. Gregory, 2462
Schoenhals, G. Roger, 3020
Scott, Leland, 3123, 3124, 3125, 3126

Scroggs, Robin, 3102
Searles, John E., 2101
Seifert, Harvey, 2437, 3363
Sell, Alan P. F., 2258
Selleck, J. Brian, 2463
Semmel, Bernard, 2037
Shaw, Anna H., 2144, 2145
Shawchuck, Norman, 2478, 2479
Sheldon, Henry C., 3152
Sherman, David, 4019
Shinn, Asa, 3130, 3136
Shipley, David C., 3127, 3128
Shipps, Howard E., 3223
Shockley, Grant S., 2171, 2210, 7013
Short, Roy H., 2077, 3305, 3306
Simpson, Matthew, 1027
Simpson, Robert Drew, 2096
Sizer, Sandra, 2389
Sledge, Robert Watson, 2015
Smith, Amanda B., 2146, 2147
Smith, Donald B., 2103
Smith, George, 3144
Smith, J. Warren, 2544
Smith, Timothy L., 2341, 2342, 2343
Smith, Warren T., 2100, 2172, 2173
Snyder, Howard A., 2198, 3250, 3251, 3252
Solomon, Martha, 2143
Southon, Arthur E., 2052
Spellman, Norman W., 2118
Spencer, Jon Michael, 2390, 2419
Stacey, John, 3071
Staples, Rob L., 3313
Starkey, Lycurgus M., 3072
Steele, Daniel, 3091, 3135, 3158
Steinmetz, David C., 3287
Stephens, Peter, 2078
Stevens, Thelma, 2438, 2509
Stoeffler, F. Ernest, 3129
Stokes, Mack B., 2199, 3103
Stookey, Laurence H., 3329, 3343
Strickland, William P., 3087
Strong, James, 1026
Summers, Thomas O., 3089, 3154
Suzuki, Lester E., 2187

Swain, Clara A., 2148
Swann, Darius L., 2527
Sweet, William W., 2006, 2007
Sweet, Leonard I., 2344
Swenson, Sally, 2131
Swift, Wesley F., 2020
Switzer, David K., 2361
Switzer, Shirley, 2361
Synan, Vinson, 2345
Taggart, Norman E., 2021
Tamez, Elsa, 2065
Taylor, David L., 2538
Taylor, Prince A., Jr., 2120
Telford, John, 3024
Templin, J. Alton, 3232
Terry, Milton S., 3160
Thomas, Hilah F., 2498
Thomas, James S., 2174
Thomas, Norman E., 2110
Thomas, Paul W., 2346
Thompson, Bard, 3237
Thorsen, Donald A., 3073
Thrift, Minton, 2106
Thumma, Scott L., 2428
Thurian, Max, 2282
Tigert, John J., 4020
Tillett, Wilbur F., 3168
Trickett, David, 2464
Tucker, Karen B. Westerfield, 2539
Tuell, Jack M., 2274, 4004, 7022
Turner, George A., 3179
Turner, John M., 2022
Tuttle, Robert G., Jr., 2200, 2303, 3074
Tyson, John R., 3034, 3075
Vernon, Walter N., 2425
Vickers, John A., 1018, 2090, 5007
Vincent, John H., 3092, 3096
Wade, William N., 2540
Wagner, James K., 2312
Wainwright, Geoffrey, 2230, 2260, 2261, 2271, 3195, 3344
Wakefield, Gordon, 2465, 2466
Wakefield, Samuel, 3145
Wakeley, J. B., 2084
Walker, Alan, 2061
Wallis, Charles L., 2088

Walls, Francine E., 2347
Walsh, John D., 2029, 2439
Waltz, Alan K., 1020
Ward, Alfred Dudley, 2440
Ward, W. Reginald, 3028
Ware, Thomas, 2124
Warner, Wellman J., 2038
Warren, James I., 2391
Washburn, Paul, 2231
Watley, William D., 2541
Watson, David L., 2220, 2221, 2222, 2223, 3203
Watson, Philip S., 3035
Watson, Richard, 3084, 3085, 3132
Wearmouth, Robert F., 2039
Werner, Julia S., 2040
Wesley, Susanna, 2473
Weyer, Michel, 2079, 3076, 3234
Whaling, Frank, 2475, 3036, 7020
Wheatley, Richard, 2141
Whedon, Daniel D., 3088, 3090, 3146
Wheeler, Henry, 3162
White, Charles E., 2142
White, James F., 2214, 2215, 2216, 2217, 2517, 2542, 3315
White, Susan J., 2217
White, Woodie W., 2126
Whyman, Henry C., 2099, 2292
Wilke, Richard B., 2305
Will, Herman, 2447
Willard, Frances, 2150
Williams, William H., 2012, 2306, 3336, 3337, 3338, 3347, 3354
Wills, David W., 2169
Wilson, Kenneth B., 3006
Wilson, Robert L., 2306, 4024
Wilson, Robert W., 2448
Wimberly, Anne S., 2291
Wimberly, Edward P., 2476
Winchell, Alexander, 3149
Wogaman, J. Philip, 3364, 3365
Woo, Wesley S., 2188
Wynkoop, Mildred B., 3189
Yeager, Dick, 3296, 3297, 3307
Yoder, Don, 2392
Young, Carlton R., 2372, 2393